Digital Food

This book explores the new theoretical and political questions raised by food TV's digital transformation.

Bringing together analyses of food media texts and platform infrastructures—from streaming and catch-up TV to YouTube and Facebook food videos—it shows how new textual conventions, algorithmic practices, and market logics have redrawn the boundaries of food TV and altered the cultural place of food, and food media, in a digital era. With case studies of new and rerun television and emerging online genres, *Digital Food TV* considers what food television means at the current moment—a time when on-screen digital content is rapidly proliferating and televisual platforms and technologies are undergoing significant change.

This book will appeal to students and scholars of food studies, television studies, and digital media studies.

Michelle Phillipov is a Senior Lecturer in Media at the University of Adelaide. Her research explores the role of food media in shaping public debate, media and food industry practices, and consumer politics. She is an author or editor of five books, including *Media and Food Industries: The New Politics of Food*, *Alternative Food Politics: From the Margins to the Mainstream* (with Katherine Kirkwood), and *Fats: A Global History*.

Routledge Focus on Television Studies

The Evolution of Black Women in Television
Mammies, Matriarchs and Mistresses
Imani M. Cheers

Heroism, Celebrity and Therapy in Nurse Jackie
Christopher Pullen

Re-scheduling Television in the Digital Era
Hanne Bruun

Digital Food TV
The Cultural Place of Food in a Digital Era
Michelle Phillipov

Digital Food TV
The Cultural Place of Food in a Digital Era

Michelle Phillipov

Routledge
Taylor & Francis Group
LONDON AND NEW YORK

First published 2023
by Routledge
4 Park Square, Milton Park, Abingdon, Oxon OX14 4RN
and by Routledge
605 Third Avenue, New York, NY 10158
Routledge is an imprint of the Taylor & Francis Group, an informa business

© 2023 Michelle Phillipov

The right of Michelle Phillipov to be identified as author of this work has been asserted in accordance with sections 77 and 78 of the Copyright, Designs and Patents Act 1988.

All rights reserved. No part of this book may be reprinted or reproduced or utilised in any form or by any electronic, mechanical, or other means, now known or hereafter invented, including photocopying and recording, or in any information storage or retrieval system, without permission in writing from the publishers.

Trademark notice: Product or corporate names may be trademarks or registered trademarks, and are used only for identification and explanation without intent to infringe.

British Library Cataloguing-in-Publication Data
A catalogue record for this book is available from the British Library

Library of Congress Cataloging-in-Publication Data
Names: Phillipov, Michelle, author.
Title: Digital food TV : the cultural place of food in a digital era / Michelle Phillipov.
Description: Abingdon, Oxon ; New York : Routledge, 2023. | Series: Routledge focus on television studies | Includes bibliographical references and index. |
Identifiers: LCCN 2022033740 (print) | LCCN 2022033741 (ebook) | ISBN 9781032200323 (hardback) | ISBN 9781032200330 (paperback) | ISBN 9781003261940 (ebook)
Subjects: LCSH: Food on television. | Digital television. | Food—Political aspects. | Streaming video. | Internet television.
Classification: LCC PN1992.8.F66 P45 2023 (print) | LCC PN1992.8.F66 (ebook) | DDC 791.45/6564—dc23
LC record available at https://lccn.loc.gov/2022033740
LC ebook record available at https://lccn.loc.gov/2022033741

ISBN: 9781032200323 (hbk)
ISBN: 9781032200330 (pbk)
ISBN: 9781003261940 (ebk)

DOI: 10.4324/9781003261940

Typeset in Times New Roman
by codeMantra

Contents

Acknowledgements   vii

Introduction: Digital platforms and televisual food   1

1 Re-reading televisual flow: The politics of reruns on catch-up TV   18

2 Streaming reality: Neoliberal subjectivities, aspirational labour, and Netflix food programming   41

3 Affect switches: Affective capture and market logics in online food videos   65

4 Technologies of intimacy: Reimagining broadcast food TV in the pandemic   87

Conclusion: Television and the politics of digital food   108

Index   113

Acknowledgements

An earlier version of Chapter 2 was published in *Communication Research and Practice* (vol. 8, no. 2) under the title 'Loving neoliberalism? Digital labour and aspirational work on streaming food TV'.

Thanks to Alexander Beare and Joanne Hollows for their generous feedback on chapter drafts (Chapters 1 and 4, respectively); to Christine Knight for the thorough edit; and to Karen Gillen for the preparation of the index.

Introduction
Digital platforms and televisual food

After dominating broadcast and cable television schedules for much of the 2000s, food TV has more recently found a range of new lives in non-linear, digital forms of production and circulation. In much the same way that it once provided a salve to struggling broadcast and cable industries (Oren 2013; Phillipov 2017: 2), food content is now proliferating on digital platforms, with both new and old food offerings becoming staples of streaming services, catch-up TV, and social media. Netflix, in particular, has made significant investments in originally produced food programming in recent years (Phillipov 2022), while rerun food content continues to bolster the back catalogues of online streaming and catch-up services. Professional, semi-professional, and amateur food content produced for YouTube, TikTok, Facebook, and Instagram is also booming, with 'food' consistently outperforming most other industry categories for both audience and brand engagement (Cucu 2022).

Food television's shift away from linear schedules to "interactive, curated databases" (Lobato 2018: 243; see also Lotz 2017: 23) has seen food programming take on new forms, with older content—produced in response to earlier industrial conditions and constraints—reappearing in new contexts. These have contributed to (re)shaping the types of food content that are produced and promoted, while changing how the meanings, politics, and affects of this content are to be understood. For example, a YouTube cooking channel may adopt conventions from earlier "stand-and-stir" (Strange 1998) television cookery programs, or a Netflix Original show may mimic tropes that originated in broadcast reality formats—but the industry and audience practices and algorithmic and market logics that underpin newer digital forms mean that the powers and pleasures of individual programs may not necessarily conform to our earlier scholarly understandings. The sheer proliferation of content online disrupts many of

DOI: 10.4324/9781003261940-1

2 *Introduction*

our typical understandings of what food TV 'is' and how it operates as a textual and cultural form, while emerging industry drivers are shaping the content and production practices of television in substantially new ways.

This book is about the changing textual, cultural, and industrial contexts in which digital food TV now operates. It explores the ways in which television's digital transformation has redrawn the boundaries of food TV, the relationship between 'new' and 'old' televisual content, and its operation and circulation on digital platforms. Earlier studies of food television have typically focused on broadcast and cable programming, approaching texts as barometers of social, cultural, and economic imperatives both within and outside the television industry. Scholars have revealed, for example, the ways in which food programming aligns with and perpetuates neoliberal ideologies (Hearn 2008; Ouellette & Hay 2008; Redden 2018) and inequalities based on gender or class (Leer 2017; Skeggs & Wood 2011; Swenson 2009). Others have considered food television as a site for the advancement of an alternative food politics, including through explicit activism (Bell & Hollows 2011; Hollows & Jones 2010) and the promotion of ethical consumption (Lewis 2008b; Phillipov 2016).

However, as Deborah Lupton has put it, "academic interest in *digital* food cultures has had something of a slow start" (2020b: 3, emphasis added), and the scholarly literature on digital food media remains limited despite some growing interest since 2018 (Leer & Krogager 2021: 1).[1] Scholars in the emerging field of digital food studies have considered the role of the digital in shaping the performance of online food identities for established food celebrities, newer lifestyle 'influencers', and ordinary people alike (Braun & Carruthers 2020; Dejmanee 2016; Goodman & Jaworska 2020; Lupton 2020a; Middha 2018; Perrier & Swan 2020). Much of the work on these topics has emphasised the distinct affordances of social media platforms (including YouTube, Twitter, Facebook, and Instagram) in expanding the voices, debates, and practices that now constitute 'good' food—the increasing prominence of vegan diets, for example, or 'clean' eating. A growing body of work also considers the role of the digital in reshaping contemporary food activism, with scholars exploring phenomena ranging from digital 'apptivism' targeting ethical consumers (e.g. Lewis 2020) to new forms of political organising, advocacy, and campaigning (e.g. Eli et al. 2018; Friedlander & Riedy 2018; Mann 2018).

Contemporary research in digital food studies now encompasses a diversity of topics and approaches. Yet with some notable exceptions (e.g. Leer & Krogager 2021; Lewis 2020), much work in the field shares a tendency to approach digital food media as largely distinct from 'legacy' media forms. For example, Tisha Dejmanee (2016: 429, 443) describes the post-feminist play enabled by online food porn as both 'unique' to the digital contexts in which it appears and what distinguishes digital food porn from that on earlier media platforms. For Deborah Lupton (2020a), YouTube's carnivalesque food videos, which play with excessive and transgressive forms of food consumption, are likewise a product of the digital's specific affordances and repertoires: in this case, of the "more-than-representational" possibilities embedded in YouTube's participatory technologies and their capacity to generate new human–food–digital assemblages (Lupton 2020a: 36).

The tendency to approach digital food media as a significant departure from 'older' mediums and genres, while common in digital media studies more broadly (see Turner 2016), is nonetheless at odds with the growing propensity within television studies to approach platforms like YouTube as part of a continuum with earlier televisual forms (Lotz 2014; van Dijck 2013). José van Dijck (2013: 121), for example, has highlighted the "intimate connection" between television and video-sharing services such as YouTube, outlining the ways in which YouTube has increasingly become "more like television, while the television industry [has] increasingly adopted features from YouTube", the two "rapidly converging ... in terms of audience and content strategies". Amanda Lotz (2014) adopts a similarly expanded definition of 'television' in a post-network era; she discusses YouTube alongside broadcast television, streaming video on demand, and online television services.

In much the same way—given the continued expansion of digital content industries and growth in their food-related offerings—this book seeks to apply a definition of the 'televisual' that encompasses both 'traditional' and 'new' forms of on-screen food content. In doing so, it combines analyses of 'traditional' television, streaming and catch-up services, and online video, to capture more effectively current developments in on-screen food industries and the new theoretical, methodological, and political questions these raise. As this book will show, digital food TV still operates as a cultural barometer, but its politics are both similar to and different from those of earlier televisual forms. Using examples from a range of digital food texts, I argue that the politics of digital food TV is now not so much a politics of 'representation' as a politics of affect. That is, the politics of digital food TV lies not so much in its manifest textual content as in its capacity to flatten or amplify intensity. Such changes necessitate new ways of understanding the changing cultural and political 'place' of food—and food media—in a digital era, as well as sensitivity to the continuities and relationships between contemporary and earlier food media forms. However, before delving into the particulars of the case studies, this Introduction first maps the shifting industrial, ideological, and political terrain in which digital food TV now operates, the challenge this poses for an analysis of contemporary televisual texts, and the particular methods and approaches used in this book.

Food television: then and now

Although it is one of television's earliest genres (Collins 2009), food television did not attract significant scholarly attention until the early 2000s, following significant changes to the television industry during the two previous decades. Until about the 1990s, food television had typically been confined to stand-and-stir formats—what Niki Strange (1998: 301), in her influential early taxonomy, calls 'Cookery-Educative' programs. The restriction of such programs to the daytime broadcast schedule, coupled with their instructional mode of address, limited their audience primarily to women with responsibilities for daily domestic meal preparation (de Solier 2005: 469; Oren 2013: 21). In countries with long histories of public service broadcasting, such as the UK and Australia, such programming found its home primarily on public broadcast networks such as the BBC and the ABC, where it readily fit within the public broadcasters' ethos to "inform, educate and entertain" (Ashley et al. 2004: 173; de Solier 2008). In the US, the predominance of cable television saw the Food Network also finding sizeable audiences for stand-and-stir programming, albeit with a more explicitly commercial remit (Ketchum 2005).

There have been a number of important histories of these early types of cookery programs (e.g. Collins 2009). However, it was not until the lifestyle boom in the 1990s and 2000s, which saw lifestyle concerns increasingly colonise prime-time schedules, that there was sustained scholarly interest in food television. The rise of lifestyle programming contributed to what the Midlands Group characterised as the "daytime-ization of prime-time" (Moseley 2001: 32), with Jamie Oliver's first cookery program, *The Naked Chef*, frequently cited as a landmark text in this regard (Ashley et al. 2004; Hollows & Jones 2010; Moseley 2001). Such programs saw the cookery genre shift from instruction in cooking to instruction in the "art of lifestyle" (Ashley et al. 2004: 184), with cooking offered as part of an aspirational lifestyle 'package' achievable to increasingly diverse audiences.

This shift in the nature of prime-time programming has been understood as a reflection of cultural and political trends, particularly the late 20th-century rise of consumer-oriented, neoliberal modes of citizenship (Lewis 2008a; Miller 2007; see also Chapter 2). It has also been understood as driven by economic imperatives within the television industries, including the need for strategies to reduce production costs while retaining audiences and advertisers in the face of increasing competition, fragmentation, and deregulation (Waisbord 2004). Lifestyle television benefits from relatively low production costs (at least when compared with expensive scripted drama), as well as the capacity to stimulate "fixed viewer habits" by allowing new shows to be launched in close proximity to existing favourites (Ashley et al. 2004: 174). Lifestyle cookery programs also allow producers to take advantage of new opportunities for media synergy—not only through the significant international resale value of programs hosted by food celebrities like Jamie Oliver or Nigella Lawson but also through the release of cookbooks, DVDs, and food-related product lines, all coordinated via the television text (Ashley et al. 2004: 175).

It is perhaps not surprising, then, that as the dominance of broadcast and cable TV industries in Anglophone and Western European markets has waned in favour of newer forms of "Internet-distributed television" (Lotz 2017), so too has scholarly interest in food TV. Many former food television scholars, myself included, have moved away from the analysis of TV to consider multifarious forms of 'digital food'—including advertising and marketing, social media, apps, websites, and other online food texts (see also Lewis 2020). Food television scholarship continues (e.g. Leer 2017; Matwick & Matwick 2019; Smith 2020), but it has become increasingly marginal to the field of food media studies, and even recent studies tend to focus on broadcast and cable contexts. Few contemporary studies seek to grapple more fully with what food television 'is', in the current moment, as it moves into online forms.

This is significant, because scholarly interest in food television has declined at precisely the moment that television studies as a broader field has been enjoying new prominence. Growing interest in what Lotz (2014) calls television's third era—the "post-network" era—has seen a boom in scholarly accounts seeking to better understand the new cultural practices and industrial formations of contemporary TV. For example, there is now a burgeoning scholarship on Netflix and its contribution to the transformation of television industries and audiences (Jenner 2018; Lobato 2019; Lotz 2014). But although Netflix has made significant investments in food-related programming in recent years, its practices—and those of similar platforms and services—have attracted relatively little attention from food scholars (for an exception, see Binns 2018). There has been greater interest in some other areas of the post-network landscape, notably the significant expansion of food content on digital platforms like YouTube and other video-sharing sites (Braun & Carruthers 2020; Lupton 2020a), but few studies of such platforms have sought to understand these texts as specifically *televisual*. There are no studies I am aware of that consider food programming on digital services such as catch-up. This means that despite growing scholarly interest in contemporary television, recent developments in internet-distributed, post-network television have not been well accounted for in food media scholarship. However, television's transformations offer a productive opportunity to think about what food means at the present moment; how its meanings, politics, and affects are altered (or not) as televisual platforms change and expand; and how these potentially disrupt many of our conventional understandings of food TV and its industrial and cultural functions.

Reading post-network food television

The changes wrought by post-network television pose a number of theoretical and methodological challenges to food TV scholarship, just as they do for television studies more broadly (Lobato 2018; Lotz 2018; Lotz, Lobato & Thomas 2018). This necessitates revisiting—and, potentially, reorienting—some of the methodological approaches and theoretical questions that have dominated the field to date. The shifting balance of power in the television industry, away from the linear delivery of cable and broadcast television towards digital services such as Netflix, reflects profound changes in the way television is produced and distributed, as well as significant adjustments in audience practices of engaging with televisual content. The libraries of online distribution platforms—a category in which I would include both professional subscription services like Netflix and hybrid sites like YouTube—contain many more content options than would be possible for a terrestrial channel limited by a daily or weekly schedule (Lotz 2017). Moreover, the audience's capacity to watch any show at any time, combined with the expanded scope of available programs, produces an "exponential effect" (Lotz 2021: 893) on audience fragmentation and dispersal, disrupting the collective co-viewing that has long been a feature of traditional television. The lack of publicly available ratings data for most services further compounds this fragmentation, as it is rarely possible to gauge how many people are watching any specific program, or whether some programs are even being watched at all (Wayne 2022).

Together, these changes pose a number of challenges to television studies' long-held assumptions about the cultural power of television texts. The notion of television as a 'mass' medium has long been central to scholars' understanding of its cultural importance and ideological effects. Television has been distinguished by its ability to communicate ideas widely and to operate as a "cultural forum" through which dominant ideologies can be identified and worked through (Gray & Lotz 2012: 7). For most of television studies' history, critical questions about television's power and significance have depended on television's broad popularity as a measure of its cultural impact, especially for those studies that foreground analysis of television texts (Lotz 2021: 889). After all, how else do you choose some texts for analysis rather than others? Indeed, this emphasis on 'popularity' as a measure of cultural importance has been one of the key ways in which television analysis has been distinguished from that of other cognate mediums, such as literature or film, for which the 'size' of the audience has tended to matter a great deal less (Gray & Lotz 2012: 6).

Certainly, this is an approach I have used in my own work as a means of justifying the choice of texts for analysis. In my work on *MasterChef Australia*, for example, I used the show's record-breaking ratings as evidence of the importance of its representations of food to broader issues like obesity debates (Phillipov 2013b). Even in discussions of newer food television forms, such as YouTube, scholars often use viewer or subscription figures to justify a particular textual focus—for instance, *Epic Meal Time*'s seven million subscribers (Lupton 2019: 162). In such cases, popularity serves as a proxy for cultural impact: after all, if television operates as a cultural forum, then the larger the audience, the more persuasively it can be claimed that television is a site for the 'working through' of cultural ideas.

However, the fragmentation of post-network television into ever-smaller audience niches and "taste communities" (Lotz 2021: 893)—not to mention the lack of publicly available ratings data—serves to problematise claims about the cultural significance of any individual television text (or even groups of texts). As Lotz (2021: 889) puts it, television continues to hold an important place in contemporary culture, but our inability to gauge the cultural reach of individual television programs poses a significant dilemma for many of our standard methods of analysis. This has led to various attempts to find workable alternatives for cultural reach—including Lotz's (2014: 42–45) own concept of "phenomenal television", and other proxies such as media attention, critical acclaim, or level of fan activity. But each of these remains imperfect (Lotz 2021), not least because such proxies risk ignoring vast swathes of the contemporary television landscape. For example, television studies has tended to focus disproportionately on big-budget, 'prestige' programming—hence the vast number of studies on dramas such as *House of Cards* or *Orange is the New Black* compared with the more limited work on older, licensed, and/or more 'lowbrow' fare.

For some, the answer has been to move away from analyses of individual programs—what Graeme Turner (2021: 233) calls the "textualist tendency" of television studies—to focus instead on the audience practices, infrastructures, and algorithmic logics of new digital platforms. This involves combining television studies' traditional methods of analysis with digital media studies' approaches to questions of technology, interface, and experience (Lobato 2019; Lotz, Lobato & Thomas 2018: 41). It also involves putting aside media studies' "biases … toward content and programming" (Lotz, Lobato & Thomas 2018: 41) to develop more nuanced accounts of television's "cultures of use"—rather than assuming that audience practices and meanings can be 'read off' television texts (Turner 2021). Indeed, television's transformation from the linear schedule to the online database would seem not just to destabilise television studies' traditional focus on 'the popular' but also to justify a move away from studying television texts altogether. After all, if a "database is not a linear progression but rather '[a collection] of individual items, with every item possessing the same significance as any other'"—as Derek Kompare argues (2010: 82, emphasis removed), quoting Lev Manovich—then no text can be judged more meaningful than any other.

Certainly, increasing the theoretical and methodological diversity of television studies is essential in the present time of change and disruption. Current work must also be careful to avoid uncritically accepting past assumptions about television texts as straightforward 'access points' to cultural values and ideologies. However, we must also be careful not to assume that questions about textual content no longer matter, just because television's shift away from linear scheduling and publicly available ratings data makes it difficult to ascertain *which* television texts possess the greatest cultural impact or influence. After all, television texts remain a primary site of audience engagement, and their conventions are shaped by industry imperatives.

In much the same way that the needs of the broadcasting industry shaped the production conventions of earlier forms of television (for example, prescribing certain episode lengths or narrative rhythms that incorporated space for advertising and sponsorship), post-network television's different audience and financial imperatives produce, in turn, different types of content. This has been most pronounced in recent forms of television drama, where the affordances of digital television have enabled more complex, challenging forms of storytelling, and production decisions shaped by algorithmic logics (Bellanova & González Fuster 2018; Floegel 2021: 221; Hallinan & Striphas 2016: 128–129).

But we also see changes to other television genres. For example, much of the reality television on streaming services is a far cry from that which once dominated broadcast schedules. Reality TV's removal from linear scheduling not only profoundly changes the way audiences can engage with these texts—the on-demand nature means they no longer have the capacity to stimulate the "fixed viewer habits" (Ashley et al. 2004: 174) or watercooler culture they once did—but also (de-)prioritises certain types of content. Despite significant amounts of licensed content appearing on online streaming services, large swathes of the reality TV landscape are nowhere to be found, including previously very popular broadcast 'hits' (Gilbert 2019: 696). Of the reality programs that do appear, the most egregious forms of "advertainment" (Deery 2004) are typically absent. Instead, there is greater focus on easy-going, feel-good forms of storytelling (see Chapter 2). The new curation and cataloguing practices of internet-distributed TV have changed the focus and emphasis of televisual representations in some quite significant ways that are not necessarily well accounted for by our typical assumptions and frameworks of analysis.

The post-network era's transformation of television industries from a logic of scheduling to one of curation (Lotz 2018: 492) also means that television texts increasingly find meaning through juxtaposition. Around 80% of the content that Netflix users watch is discovered through its recommendation system (Floegel 2021: 211), and streaming service interfaces have the potential to bring together television texts and make connections between them that would never have occurred in a linear schedule. These new contexts can reshape the meanings of older texts, too, as they are distributed via these new methods, and (in the case of food TV, in particular) necessitate a rethinking of many of the established meanings and industrial practices we have typically associated with the medium.

Such rethinking requires a move away from many of television studies' traditional assumptions about the central importance of television's 'popularity' and 'reach'—but not necessarily that we abandon the theoretical and methodological tools provided by textual analysis. Significant continuities still exist between streaming and legacy television (Lotz 2018: 491; Sanson & Steirer 2019: 1212; Ulin 2014: 333), presenting both new and old questions for television research, which a reinvigorated focus on television texts may assist in answering. I have previously argued (Phillipov 2013a) that textual analysis has often been derided as a method of 'anecdote' or 'speculation', ill-equipped to understand what audiences actually *do* with media texts (see Turner 2021 for a recent version of this critique). Certainly, it is a method that has fallen out of favour in food media studies as the focus of work has shifted from 'traditional' to 'digital' media (Phillipov 2021). However, I would suggest that textual analysis remains useful: not to uncover 'the' meaning of a text, nor to replace study of what audiences do with media texts, but to provide an additional point of access to understand the power and affective charge of contemporary media forms (Phillipov 2013a). Such an approach involves not decontextualised 'close readings' of individual media texts, but rather properly contextual interpretations that consider both audience and industry contexts—as well as the ways in which texts move within and between media platforms, forming relationships of intertextuality and paratextuality with other media texts (Phillipov 2021).

Book structure and approach

This book adopts this kind of contextual approach in order to analyse the meanings and politics of contemporary food TV. Specifically, it seeks to identify the "moments of possibility" (Barnes 2017) that result from food TV's digital transformations, and consider what these reveal about the political power of food and food television as they move into online contexts. To do so, I approach digital food texts not just as sites of representations, but also as spaces of *affect*. I draw from Brian Massumi's (1987) approach to affect as the "ability to affect and be affected": affect is a "prepersonal intensity corresponding to the passage from one experiential state of the body to another and implying an augmentation or diminution in that body's capacity to act" (Massumi 1987: xvi). If, as I suggest in this book, the politics of digital food TV now often lies in its capacity to flatten or amplify intensity, this ideally suits an approach attuned to the operation of affect. Such an approach allows us to reframe our reading of televisual texts in ways that consider not only what the texts 'depict', but also how texts *act* upon audiences (and industries) as they move within and between platforms and services, and how such affects can be mobilised or diminished for particular ends.

Introduction 11

This book explores such questions through four case studies, each of which takes a key concept, digital platform (or group of platforms), and focal texts as its starting point. Textual examples have been drawn from a range of contexts, including Australia, the US, UK, and Asia, although choices inevitably reflect my own Antipodean location and the access (or lack of it) to specific television texts that this affords. With the notable exception of Chapter 1, which looks at Australian catch-up service SBS on Demand, the texts and platforms analysed in this book have largely been chosen for their availability across international audiences and markets. However, recognising that regional specificities can still produce distinct patterns of digital curation and circulation, texts and platforms are discussed (where relevant) with sufficient context to assist readers in regions outside my own. The cases used in *Digital Food TV* are not an attempt to be comprehensive or definitive, but a means of anchoring particular questions and arguments in specific examples. Taken together, the cases reveal the ways in which digital distribution necessitates both new and old analytical lenses, in order to capture the meanings, politics, and affects of food and food television as platforms and representations shift and evolve.

Chapter 1 reworks Raymond Williams' (1974 [2003]) concept of flow to explore the ways in which the politics of rerun food television can be altered as programs reappear on online catch-up services. Using examples of programs that have typically been understood as part of the politically progressive genre of 'eco-reality' TV, the chapter shows how the shift of such programs from broadcast schedule to online database alters the interpretations invited of their politics, and offers a range of new meanings shaped by the ordering systems of catch-up platforms. Specifically, the chapter suggests that assumptions we may once have held about how the politics of television texts 'work' may no longer hold true once texts move into digital spaces of production and circulation. In fact, I argue, once such texts are evacuated from their original broadcast contexts, there may be no natural reason that we should read them as 'political' at all.

Chapter 2 analyses cooking competition programs on online streaming services, revealing the ways in which such programs typically replace the aggressively disciplinary and pedagogical impulses of earlier forms of reality TV with more easy-going, feel-good pleasures. However, such pleasures are produced, the chapter suggests, through a persistent reframing of affective experiences of labour for both contestants and audiences. Indeed, with streaming reality's apparently

12 Introduction

'amateur' contestants expected to undertake an ever-larger share of the production and promotional work essential to reality TV—and to conceive of this work as a fun form of leisure—their labours increasingly parallel the unpaid *audience* labour now central to the infrastructures and business models of streaming platforms such as Netflix.

Chapter 3 focuses its attention on online food videos—Facebook and YouTube, in particular. Using examples from online baking videos, it departs from earlier understandings of such videos as primarily instructional, to reveal the ways in which online food content mobilises and intensifies experiences of materiality and affect. The chapter explores the ways in which online food videos bring together texts, bodies, and platforms in encounters that give rise to nascent and contingent forms of cooking and eating. These simultaneously expand the conceptual boundaries of food TV—and, indeed, those of cooking itself—highlighting the complex tensions between the user-generated and commercial agendas that underpin the production and circulation of online food texts.

If, as Chapter 3 suggests, digital food TV possesses a range of "vitalities and visceralities" (Lupton 2019: 151), the implications of which cannot always be known in advance, Chapter 4 considers some of these in the context of broadcast television. It explores the affects produced by the adoption of mobile technologies in the production of Jamie Oliver's 2020 television program *Keep Cooking and Carry On*. The chapter argues that such technologies produced feelings of intimacy and closeness during the COVID-19 pandemic, on the one hand serving to obscure and normalise Oliver's privilege, but on the other hand having the unexpected effect of forming new relationships between viewers. This highlights the extent to which the politics of digital food TV do not necessarily reside in the manifest content of texts, but in the ways in which digital food content creates points of connection and access that cannot always be anticipated in advance.

Each of the chapters, then, highlights key shifts in the political power of food television as texts move online. As the Conclusion further outlines, these shifts now necessitate an approach that considers digital food TV at the intersection of textual representations, platform infrastructures, and cultural contexts. Such an approach requires that scholars look for television's politics in different ways and in different places than we have typically done. But in doing so, we are able to see anew the 'moments of possibility' offered by both new and old food television as texts proliferate and transform on contemporary digital platforms.

Note

1 For examples of such work, see Feldman and Goodman (2021), Leer and Krogager (2021), Lewis (2020), Lewis and Phillipov (2018), Lupton and Feldman (2020), and Schneider et al. (2018).

References

Ashley, Bob, Hollows, Joanne, Jones, Steve & Taylor, Ben 2004, *Food and Cultural Studies*. Routledge: London.

Barnes, Christine 2017, 'Mediating good food and moments of possibility with Jamie Oliver: Problematizing celebrity chefs as talking labels', *Geoforum*, vol. 84, pp. 169–178. https://doi.org/10.1016/j.geoforum.2014.09.004

Bell, David & Hollows, Joanne 2011, 'From *River Cottage* to *Chicken Run*: Hugh Fearnley-Whittingstall and the class politics of ethical consumption', *Celebrity Studies*, vol. 2, no. 2, pp. 178–191. https://doi.org/10.1080/19392397.2011.574861

Bellanova, Rocco & González Fuster, Gloria 2018, 'No (big) data, no fiction? Thinking surveillance with/against Netflix'. In Ann Rudinow Sætnan, Ingrid Schneider & Nicola Green (eds), *The Politics and Policies of Big Data: Big Data Big Brother?* Routledge: London, pp. 227–246.

Binns, Daniel 2018, 'The Netflix documentary house style: Streaming TV and slow media', *Fusion Journal*, vol. 14, pp. 60–71. http://www.fusion-journal.com/the-netflix-documentary-house-style-streaming-tv-and-slow-media/

Braun, Virginia & Carruthers, Sophie 2020, 'Working at self and wellness: A critical analysis of vegan vlogs'. In Deborah Lupton & Zeena Feldman (eds), *Digital Food Cultures*. Routledge: Abingdon, pp. 82–96.

Collins, Kathleen 2009, *Watching What We Eat: The Evolution of Television Cooking Shows*. Continuum: New York.

Cucu, Elena 2022, *2022 Social Media Industry Benchmarks*, 24 February, https://www.socialinsider.io/blog/social-media-industry-benchmarks/#6. Accessed 6 April 2022.

Deery, June 2004, 'Reality TV as advertisement', *Popular Communication*, vol. 2, no. 1, pp. 1–20. https://doi.org/10.1207/s15405710pc0201_1

Dejmanee, Tisha 2016, '"Food porn" as postfeminist play: Digital femininity and the female body on food blogs', *Television & New Media*, vol. 17, no. 5, pp. 429–448. https://doi.org/10.1177/1527476415615944

de Solier, Isabelle 2005, 'TV dinners: Culinary television, education and distinction', *Continuum: Journal of Media & Cultural Studies*, vol. 19, no. 4, pp. 465–481. https://doi.org/10.1080/10304310500322727

de Solier, Isabelle 2008, 'Foodie makeovers: Public service television and lifestyle guidance'. In Gareth Palmer (ed.), *Exposing Lifestyle Television: The Big Reveal*. Ashgate: Aldershot, pp. 65–81.

Eli, Karin, Schneider, Tanja, Dolan, Catherine & Ulijaszek, Stanley 2018, 'Digital food activism: Values, expertise and modes of action'. In Tanja Schneider, Karin Eli, Catherine Dolan and Stanley Ulijaszek (eds), *Digital Food Activism*. Routledge: London, pp. 203–219.

Feldman, Zeena & Goodman, Michael K. 2021, 'Digital food culture, power and everyday life', *European Journal of Cultural Studies*, vol. 24, no. 6, pp. 1227–1242. https://doi.org/10.1177/13675494211055501

Floegel, Diana 2021, 'Labor, classification and productions of culture on Netflix', *Journal of Documentation*, vol. 77, no. 1, pp. 209–228. https://doi.org/10.1108/JD-06-2020-0108

Friedlander, Judith & Riedy, Chris 2018, 'Celebrities, credibility, and complementary frames: Raising the agenda of sustainable and other "inconvenient" food issues in social media campaigning', *Communication Research and Practice*, vol. 4, no. 3, pp. 229–245. https://doi.org/10.1080/22041451.2018.1448210

Gilbert, Anne 2019, 'Push, pull, rerun: Television reruns and streaming media', *Television & New Media*, vol. 20, no. 7, pp. 686–701. https://doi.org/10.1177/1527476419842418

Goodman, Michael K. & Jaworska, Sylvia 2020, 'Mapping digital foodscapes: Digital food influencers and the grammars of good food', *Geoforum*, vol. 117, pp. 183–193. https://doi.org/10.1016/j.geoforum.2020.09.020

Gray, Jonathan & Lotz, Amanda D. 2012, *Television Studies*. Polity: Cambridge.

Hallinan, Blake & Striphas, Ted 2016, 'Recommended for you: The Netflix Prize and the production of algorithmic culture', *New Media & Society*, vol. 18, no. 1, pp. 117–137. https://doi.org/10.1177/1461444814538646

Hearn, Alison 2008, 'Insecure: Narratives and economies of the branded self in transformation television', *Continuum: Journal of Media & Cultural Studies*, vol. 22, no. 4, pp. 495–504. https://doi.org/10.1080/10304310802189972

Hollows, Joanne & Jones, Steve 2010, '"At least he's doing something": Moral entrepreneurship and individual responsibility in *Jamie's Ministry of Food*', *European Journal of Cultural Studies*, vol. 13, no. 3, pp. 307–322. https://doi.org/10.1177/1367549410363197

Jenner, Mareike 2018, *Netflix and the Re-invention of Television*. Palgrave Macmillan: Cham.

Ketchum, Cheri 2005, 'The essence of cooking shows: How the Food Network constructs consumer fantasies', *Journal of Communication Inquiry*, vol. 29, no. 3, pp. 217–234. https://doi.org/10.1177/0196859905275972

Kompare, Derek 2010, 'Reruns 2.0: Revising repetition for multiplatform television distribution', *Journal of Popular Film and Television*, vol. 38, no. 2, pp. 79–83. https://doi.org/10.1080/01956051.2010.483353

Leer, Jonathan 2017, 'Gender and food television: A transnational perspective on the gendered identities of televised celebrity chefs'. In Kathleen LeBesco & Peter Naccarato (eds), *The Bloomsbury Handbook of Food and Popular Culture*. Bloomsbury: London, pp. 13–26.

Leer, Jonatan & Krogager, Stinne Gunder Strøm 2021, *Research Methods in Digital Food Studies*. Routledge: London.

Lewis, Tania 2008a, *Smart Living: Lifestyle Media and Popular Expertise*. Peter Lang: New York.

Lewis, Tania 2008b, 'Transforming citizens? Green politics and ethical consumption on lifestyle television', *Continuum: Journal of Media & Cultural Studies*, vol. 22, no. 2, pp. 227–240. https://doi.org/10.1080/10304310701864394

Lewis, Tania 2020, *Digital Food: From Paddock to Platform*. Bloomsbury Academic: London.
Lewis, Tania & Phillipov, Michelle 2018, 'Food/media: Eating, cooking, and provisioning in a digital world', *Communication Research and Practice*, vol. 4, no. 3, pp. 207–211. https://doi.org/10.1080/22041451.2018.1482075
Lobato, Ramon 2018, 'Rethinking international TV flows research in the age of Netflix', *Television & New Media*, vol. 19, no. 3, pp. 241–256. https://doi.org/10.1177/1527476417708245
Lobato, Ramon 2019, *Netflix Nations: The Geography of Digital Distribution*. New York University Press: New York.
Lotz, Amanda 2014, *The Television Will Be Revolutionized* (2nd edition). New York University Press: New York.
Lotz, Amanda 2017, *Portals: A Treatise on Internet-Distributed Television*. University of Michigan Press: Ann Arbor.
Lotz, Amanda 2018, 'Evolution or revolution? Television in transformation', *Critical Studies in Television: The International Journal of Television Studies*, vol. 13, no. 4, pp. 491–494. https://doi.org/10.1177/1749602018796757
Lotz, Amanda 2021, 'Unpopularity and cultural power in the age of Netflix: New questions for cultural studies' approaches to television texts', *European Journal of Cultural Studies*, vol. 24, no. 4, pp. 887–900. https://doi.org/10.1177/1367549421994578
Lotz, Amanda, Lobato, Ramon & Thomas, Julian 2018, 'Internet-distributed television research: A provocation', *Media Industries*, vol. 5, no. 2. https://doi.org/10.3998/mij.15031809.0005.203
Lupton, Deborah 2019, 'Vitalities and visceralities: Alternative body/food politics in digital media'. In Michelle Phillipov & Katherine Kirkwood (eds), *Alternative Food Politics: From the Margins to the Mainstream*. Routledge: London, pp. 151–168.
Lupton, Deborah 2020a, 'Carnivalesque food videos: Excess, gender and affect on YouTube'. In Deborah Lupton & Zeena Feldman (eds), *Digital Food Cultures*. Routledge: Abingdon, pp. 35–49.
Lupton, Deborah 2020b, 'Understanding digital food cultures'. In Deborah Lupton & Zeena Feldman (eds), *Digital Food Cultures*. Routledge: Abingdon, pp. 1–16.
Lupton, Deborah & Feldman, Zeena (eds) 2020, *Digital Food Cultures*. Routledge: Abingdon.
Mann, Alana 2018, 'Hashtag activism and the right to food in Australia'. In Tanja Schneider, Karin Eli, Catherine Dolan and Stanley Ulijaszek (eds), *Digital Food Activism*. Routledge: London, pp. 168–184.
Matwick, Kelsi & Matwick, Keri 2019, *Food Discourse of Celebrity Chefs of Food Network*. Palgrave Macmillan: Cham.
Massumi, Brian 1987, 'Notes on the translation and acknowledgements'. In Gilles Deleuze & Felix Guattari, *A Thousand Plateaus*. University of Minnesota Press: Minneapolis, pp. xvii–xx.
Middha, Bhavna 2018, 'Everyday digital engagements: Using food selfies on Facebook to explore eating practices', *Communication Research and Practice*, vol. 4, no. 3, pp. 291–306. https://doi.org/10.1080/22041451.2018.1476796

Miller, Toby 2007, *Cultural Citizenship: Cosmopolitanism, Consumerism and Television in a Neoliberal Age*. Temple University Press: Philadelphia, PA.

Moseley, Rachel 2001, '"Real lads do cook....but some things are still hard to talk about": The gendering of 8–9', *European Journal of Cultural Studies*, vol. 4, no. 1, pp. 32–39. https://doi.org/10.1177/136754940100400102

Oren, Tasha 2013, 'On the line: Format, cooking and competition as television values', *Critical Studies in Television*, vol. 8, no. 2, pp. 20–35. https://doi.org/10.7227/CST.8.2.3

Ouellette, Laurie & Hay, James 2008, *Better Living Through Reality TV: Television and Post-Welfare Citizenship*. Blackwell: Malden, MA.

Perrier, Maud & Swan, Elaine 2020, '"Crazy for carcass": Sarah Wilson, foodie-waste femininity and digital whiteness'. In Deborah Lupton & Zeena Feldman (eds), *Digital Food Cultures*. Routledge: Abingdon, pp. 129–144.

Phillipov, Michelle 2013a, 'In defense of textual analysis: Resisting methodological hegemony in media and cultural studies', *Critical Studies in Media Communication*, vol. 30, no. 3, pp. 209–223. https://doi.org/10.1080/15295036.2011.639380

Phillipov, Michelle 2013b, '*Master*ing obesity: *MasterChef Australia* and the resistance to public health nutrition', *Media, Culture & Society*, vol. 35, no. 4, pp. 506–515. https://doi.org/10.1177/0163443712474615

Phillipov, Michelle 2016, 'Escaping to the country: Media, nostalgia, and the new food industries', *Popular Communication*, vol. 14, no. 2, pp. 111–122. https://doi.org/10.1080/15405702.2015.1084620

Phillipov, Michelle 2017, *Media and Food Industries: The New Politics of Food*. Palgrave Macmillan: Cham.

Phillipov, Michelle 2021, 'Textual analysis in digital food studies: New approaches to old methods'. In Jonatan Leer & Stinne Gunder Strøm Krogager (eds), *Research Methods in Digital Food Studies*. Routledge: London, pp. 15–27.

Phillipov, Michelle 2022, 'Loving neoliberalism? Digital labour and aspirational work on streaming food TV', *Communication Research and Practice*, vol. 8, no. 2, pp. 152–165. https://doi.org/10.1080/22041451.2022.2057270

Redden, Guy 2018, 'Is reality TV neoliberal?', *Television & New Media*, vol. 19, no. 5, pp. 399–414. https://doi.org/10.1177/1527476417728377

Sanson, Kevin & Steirer, Gregory 2019, 'Hulu, streaming, and the contemporary television ecosystem', *Media, Culture & Society*, vol. 41, no. 8, pp. 1210–1227. https://doi.org/10.1177/0163443718823144

Schneider, Tanja, Eli, Karin, Dolan, Catherine & Ulijaszek, Stanley (eds) 2018, *Digital Food Activism*. Routledge: London.

Skeggs, Beverley & Wood, Helen (eds) 2011, *Reality Television and Class*. Palgrave Macmillan: London.

Smith, Gilly 2020, *Taste and the TV Chef: How Storytelling Can Save the Planet*. Intellect: Bristol.

Introduction 17

Strange, Niki 1998, 'Perform, educate, entertain: Ingredients of the cookery programme genre'. In Christine Geraghty & David Lusted (eds), *The Television Studies Book*. London: Arnold, pp. 301–312.

Swenson, Rebecca 2009, 'Domestic divo? Televised treatments of masculinity, femininity and food', *Critical Studies in Media Communication*, vol. 26, no. 1, pp. 36–53. https://doi.org/10.1080/15295030802684034

Turner, Graeme 2016, *Re-inventing the Media*. Routledge: London.

Turner, Graeme 2021, 'Television studies, we need to talk about "binge-viewing"', *Television & New Media*, vol. 22, no. 3, pp. 228–240. https://doi.org/10.1177/1527476419877041

Ulin, Jeff 2014, *The Business of Media Distribution*. Focal: New York.

van Dijck, José 2013, *The Culture of Connectivity: A Critical History of Social Media*. Oxford University Press: Oxford.

Waisbord, Silvio 2004, 'McTV: Understanding the global popularity of television formats', *Television & New Media*, vol. 5, no. 4, pp. 359–383. https://doi.org/10.1177/1527476404268922

Wayne, Michael L. 2022, 'Netflix audience data, streaming industry discourse, and the emerging realities of "popular" television', *Media, Culture & Society*, vol. 44, no. 2, pp. 193–209. https://doi.org/10.1177/01634437211022723

Williams, Raymond 1974 [2003], *Television: Technology and Cultural Form*. Routledge: London.

1 Re-reading televisual flow
The politics of reruns on catch-up TV

While the primary focus of *Digital Food TV* is on new forms of food content, this first chapter considers the new lives of *old* television as it moves into online distribution. As Anne Gilbert (2019: 686, 687) argues, scholars of digital television have paid "outsized attention ... to original programming native to [digital] platforms", despite the fact that around 80% of viewing on digital streaming platforms is licensed (rather than original) content. Online distributors' reliance on licensed content has attributed new economic value and cultural significance to programs that may otherwise have been relegated to obscurity (Gilbert 2019: 696). This is especially true of food TV: programs originally designed for broadcast or cable television are now increasingly in demand as inexpensive fodder for content-hungry digital services. It is important to understand the significance of previously aired content for digital platforms not only because online distribution has successfully helped to create new markets for old television but also because the new contexts in which this content appears challenge a number of our previous analytical assumptions about food TV—particularly how we understand the political possibilities of certain types of televisual texts.

In order to explore food television's shifting meanings and politics as shows are circulated in new contexts, this chapter considers two popular television series, *River Cottage* and *Gourmet Farmer*, that have typically been read as 'political'—specifically, as advancing an environmental politics through their narratives of self-sufficiency. The *River Cottage* series, first aired in 1999, followed the downshifting of Hugh Fearnley-Whittingstall, a British journalist and food writer, as he relocated from London to a small farm in Dorset in South West England. The show was a ratings hit for Channel 4 (Britain's publicly owned, commercially funded broadcaster), resulting in more than ten series, sales in international territories, and international versions of

DOI: 10.4324/9781003261940-2

the *River Cottage* franchise. *Gourmet Farmer*, released in 2010, is the story of Matthew Evans, a food critic who gave up his job in Australia's capital to move to rural Tasmania. Now in its sixth series, the show was an unexpected success for Australia's multicultural public broadcaster SBS, with broadcast episodes of some series attracting up to 700,000 viewers (SBS 2013: 69)—no small feat for a niche public broadcaster with Australia's smallest audience share. Since their original televisual broadcasts, both shows have found new homes on digital catch-up TV, with the potential to significantly extend the lives, audiences, and reach of older programs like these. This chapter considers the new 'place' of these programs on one such catch-up service, Australia's SBS On Demand, which has increasingly turned to (rerun) culinary television in response to growing funding pressure and competition in the Australian television market (SBS 2015). SBS has significantly expanded its digital offerings in recent years—increasingly as an alternative, not simply a supplement, to its broadcast services—and, at the time of writing, holds the largest share of Australia's digital, free-to-air market (SBS 2020a: 6).

As a result, SBS On Demand offers an ideal case through which to explore the significance of new forms of online distribution for the circulation and reception of older televisual content. The chapter begins by revisiting Raymond Williams' (1974 [2003]) concept of televisual flow, a concept initially developed to understand television programming in a broadcast era, but potentially useful for understanding the meanings and ordering systems of online platforms. I consider how the SBS online interface, like those of other catch-up and streaming services, produces groupings of television texts (by genre, theme, etc.) that create digitally specific forms of flow, simultaneously decontextualising and recontextualising older forms of food content. The chapter goes on to apply Williams' concept of flow in a re-reading of earlier scholarship on *River Cottage* and *Gourmet Farmer*, focusing on narratives of rural self-sufficiency and livestock production, in particular. I suggest that there is no necessary reason why we should continue to interpret these texts as reflecting an (explicit or potential) environmental or sustainability politics, as scholarship on both series has previously done. Instead, as online databases' new forms of flow suspend traditional forms of televisual temporality and remove television texts from their original broadcast contexts, we may be just as likely to read these series as feel-good travelogues. My readings of *River Cottage* and *Gourmet Farmer* and their online contexts are potentially idiosyncratic: others' interpretations of the shows might be different, and my experiences of flow might differ from those of viewers in other locations and at other times. Nonetheless, these readings highlight the need to rethink some of our assumptions about the politics of digital food TV, where and how these occur, and how these politics might be altered as viewing and distribution contexts change.

Reruns and temporality

Reruns of older programs have long represented a significant proportion of broadcast and cable television schedules (Gilbert 2019: 688). Indeed, as Derek Kompare argues in *Rerun Nation*, throughout much of the medium's history reruns have been "one of the primary products of television, fueling unprecedented industrial synergies and corporate branding ... and fostering experiences and practices of television structured around continual repetition" (Kompare 2005: xi). Through syndication, rerun programs' lives and audiences can be extended as they are sold across domestic and international markets. As a viewing experience, however, reruns have generally been understood as temporally bounded. In the traditional program schedule, reruns often appear at certain times (e.g. late afternoon, late night) and are clearly designated as *repeats*. The popularity of reruns has often been understood as a reflection of the cultural moment: for example, the popularity of televisual repeats from the 1950s and 1960s during the turbulent years of the 1970s has been seen to reflect a desire for stability and nostalgia for simpler times (Kompare 2005: 103). In these respects, television programs can be seen as "semiotic capsules of the recent past", and this sense of historicity has shaped the terms in which they are typically circulated and received: as 'classics', as 'cultural memory', as 'national heritage', and so on (Kompare 2005: 103).

However, television's shift from linear delivery to searchable, online archives significantly disrupts the role of old content as it moves to new platforms. In an influential early formulation, Raymond Williams (1974 [2003]) argued that the distinctiveness of television as a medium lies not so much in the characteristics of individual programs as in the viewer's experience of the *flow* of material on screen. "Planned flow", he wrote, is "perhaps the defining characteristic of broadcasting"— with the sequence of programs and advertising designed to keep viewers watching programming *blocks* (e.g. "an evening's viewing") rather than single *shows* (Williams 1974 [2003]: 86, 93). This, for Williams, necessitates moving analyses beyond individual television texts to consider how a show can affect the meanings of those preceding or following it, for example, or how the choice and content of advertisements can shape and alter meaning within programs.

The broadcast era is littered with examples of flow in practice. For example, networks have tended to launch new programs to capitalise on audiences for current hits: NBC's habit of following the hugely successful *Seinfeld* with newer, untested sitcoms is a frequently cited instance of how (often second-rate) offerings can benefit from the atmosphere, viewership, and 'flow' created by more popular texts (Gray & Lotz 2012: 128). Broadcast scheduling of reality and lifestyle television has similarly been designed to create predictable schedules in primetime (Moseley 2001) and allow new shows to be launched in close proximity to existing favourites (Ashley et al. 2004: 174). However, streaming television's disruption of the linear schedule creates an altogether different kind of flow. The online catalogues of internet-distributed television are distinctly different from the linear schedules of the broadcast and cable eras, and they create distinctly different viewing experiences (Lobato 2018: 243). The libraries of online distributors may be dominated by content that originated on legacy television (Gilbert 2019: 686), but these programs can no longer be straightforwardly classified as *reruns*. This is because, Kompare (2010: 81–82) argues, "reruns" signify a "time bound word tracing a linear chronology"; in contrast, online television's *files* (Kompare's preferred term) are "arranged spatially and available at any time". Michael Curtin (2009: 19) has described digital delivery as a "media matrix" of non-linear, decentralised transmission, through which users cultivate diverse and flexible experiences based on their individual preferences and use patterns. This matrix shifts the experience of previously aired content from "push" to "pull", fundamentally reconfiguring the way that viewers engage with older programming (Gilbert 2019: 688).

If the flow of broadcast television created a kind of narrative for viewers, with each individual text shaping the meaning of those before and after, the databases of internet-distributed TV would seem to abandon conventional notions of narrative altogether. As Lev Manovich (2002: 225) puts it:

> As a cultural form, the database represents the world as a list of items, and it refuses to order this list. In contrast, a narrative creates a cause-and-effect trajectory of seemingly unordered items... Therefore, database and narrative are natural enemies. Competing for the same territory of human culture, each claim is an exclusive right to make meaning out of the world.

Some have countered that the algorithms of streaming television help to counterbalance and steer the database in ways that give it order and meaning for audiences (Bellanova & González Fuster 2018; Cox 2018). But even without algorithms, databases produce their own forms of meaning-making, and their interfaces help to bring together disparate texts into potentially identifiable narratives.

We can see this occurring especially clearly in the food programming on SBS On Demand. Scholars have tended to see catch-up services as more closely linked to the practices of legacy television than to those of contemporary streaming platforms (Gilbert 2019: 690; Jenner 2016: 261). In some ways this is true: with few exceptions, catch-up television remains largely dependent on advertising and tends to focus on national audiences and markets (Lobato 2018). The latter is certainly the case for SBS, which is accessible only to Australian-based viewers and whose Charter requires that its programming reflect Australia's multicultural society (SBS 2020b). However, catch-up services are also distinct from legacy television in several key ways. Catch-up television typically presents programming in catalogues, not schedules, and the interfaces of most major services increasingly look and operate much like those of streaming platforms, albeit without the sophisticated algorithms. The SBS On Demand interface, for example, replicates many aspects of the design of commercial streaming services, including an 'auto-play' feature and horizontal tiles that group television programs by genre or category (e.g. 'news and current affairs', 'historical drama', 'Nordic noir', 'food'). Some categories that appear on the landing page as broad genres (such as 'food') are further broken down into subcategories (like 'baking at home', 'armchair travel', and 'flavours of Australia') when the user clicks through, further mimicking streamers' propensity for specialised categories and sub-genres.

As is typical of other online databases (Hoyt 2014: 200; Lobato 2018: 242), the content on SBS On Demand varies frequently as licensing agreements change and shift. As a relatively inexpensive form of programming, food television is often licensed in bundles. This means that SBS On Demand's food offerings may at one time be dominated by US Food Network reruns, while at another time there may be a glut of British content. This results in viewers being offered programs they may not ordinarily encounter, and which may never have appeared alongside each other (or, indeed, at all) in the linear broadcast schedule. As Kompare's definitional shift from "reruns" to "files" suggests, online platforms produce specific forms of temporality that shape the production and organisation of meaning. For Rebecca Coleman (2018), online portals produce specifically *present* forms of temporality. Streaming television, in particular, produces a "suspended or expanded present", reducing spatial and temporal distance, and creating a seemingly endless flow of content available at any time (Coleman 2018: 600, 602). On-demand viewing, she argues, temporally suspends progression from past to present to future: it allows the present to be "at once moving (on)—to the next episode in a series, for instance—and suspended or expanded—by bracketing off the speed of life and the near future" through immersive and affective experiences like binge viewing (Coleman 2018: 613, 614). Streaming television's perpetual present may be especially amplified on a platform such as SBS On Demand, which replicates many of the infrastructural features of streaming platforms but (unlike most other platforms) does not identify the production date of its programs. Instead, programs released over a period of more than 20 years sit side by side without historical or temporal context.

Reimagining the 'good life'

Such atemporality, then, necessitates a different way of understanding the meaning and significance of television texts than has been typical of dominant scholarly understandings of food TV. As discussed in more detail in Chapter 2, food and lifestyle television have typically been read as reflections of their historical moment—as "informed by a particular televisual political economy and temporality", in the words of Wendy Parkins and Geoffrey Craig (2011: 191). The historical specificity of food and lifestyle television is what has led, for example, to them being understood as responses to the global rise of neoliberal, consumer-oriented modes of citizenship (Lewis 2008a; Miller 2007). Such an approach has contributed to scholarly concentration on a range of aspects of food and lifestyle television, including their neoliberal investment in the entrepreneurial self and focus on individual lifestyle 'choices' as methods for investing in ethical, social, and civic concerns (Bell & Hollows 2011; Lewis 2012; Littler 2008). Considered from this perspective, lifestyle television can be conceived as a source of re-enchantment—a roadmap for 'living well' within late modernity through "less alienated, more engaged modes of consumption" (Lewis 2008b: 232; see also Versteegen 2010: 459–460). In food television, these concerns have found a variety of modes of expression, often centring around ideas of authenticity, provenance, tradition, and/or localness as inherent 'goods' of food production and as methods of reconnecting urban consumers with the sources of their food (Phillipov 2017).

Thus, much network-era food television echoes the politics of "embeddedness, trust and place" (Goodman 2003: 1) characteristic of alternative food practices. Television's "foodie boom" in the first decades of the millennium (de Solier 2008) emerged out of a broader intensification of media interest in food occurring at the same time, and driven by growing media and consumer concerns about the deleterious impacts of industrial food systems. During the preceding decades, disease outbreaks linked to large-scale production and supply chains, including 'mad cow' disease in the UK and deadly *E. coli* outbreaks in the US, had drawn public attention to the risks of large-scale, industrial production methods (Pollan 2006; Schlosser 2002). Declining consumer trust in corporate agriculture became a key driver of growth in more 'trustworthy' alternatives, including the expansion of farmers' markets and community supported agriculture schemes, as well as the reinvigoration of local, artisanal production (Campbell 2009). In the US, for example, farmers' markets experienced nearly a five-fold increase between 1994 and 2019 (Warsaw et al. 2021). In Australia, the number of farmers' markets more than doubled between 2004 and 2015 (Nelan, Jansson & Szabo 2017), driven largely by their capacity to generate more personalised, transparent, and trustworthy relationships between producer and consumer than is possible within larger-scale systems (Hinrichs 2003).

Appearing around the same time, Michael Pollan's bestselling books *The Omnivore's Dilemma* (2006) and *In Defence of Food* (2008) delivered scathing attacks on an industrial food system driven solely by the pursuit of cheapness and profit. Combining a blueprint for 'good' eating with exposés of the devastating health, environmental, and animal welfare consequences of industrial food, Pollan (2008: 1) encouraged consumers to avoid the highly processed "edible food-like substances" of the industrial food industry and to embrace scratch cooking with well-raised ingredients of known provenance. His books contrasted horrific images of "agribusiness apocalypse" (Newbury 2012: 87) with bucolic alternatives of investing in local communities, building direct relationships with farmers, and seeing for oneself the conditions under which animals and crops are grown (Pollan 2006: 258). In Australia and the UK, where television chefs have held disproportionate influence in debates about food politics (Phillipov 2017: 54; Versteegen 2010: 447), concerns about industrial food primarily manifested by way of food television. In the first decade of the millennium, a proliferation of food television shows—ranging from *The Cook and the Chef* and *Paddock to Plate* in Australia to *The Hairy Bikers Food Tour of Britain* in the UK—presented audiences with models of production, preparation, and consumption that stood in contrast to the "massified, supermarketized world of industrial food" (Lewis 2008b: 232). The narrative emphasis of such programs was as much on the sourcing of produce as the cooking of dishes. Programs generally featured hosts sourcing food directly from producers in bucolic surrounds. For example, *The Cook and the Chef*, set in South Australia's picturesque Barossa Valley and hosted by Maggie Beer and Simon Bryant, centred on their interactive encounters with a range of Australian food sellers, in which they sampled produce, discussed production techniques, and encouraged audiences to "always use what's fresh and nearest to your doorstep" (Beer qtd. in Lewis 2008b: 233). By the mid-2000s, this focus on sourcing produce from local producers had become almost *de rigueur* on food television, and served to relocate 'alternative' food practices from the fringes of food activism to the 'mainstream' of food media (Phillipov 2019).

Though not usually explicitly stated as such within the programs themselves, the trope of local transparency and 'connection' that came to dominate food television in the 2000s and 2010s has been generally understood by scholars as a response to the wider food systems debates and concerns that were occurring at the time. For example, explaining the appeal of food programming in the mid-2000s, Heinrich Versteegen (2010: 459) describes food television's interest in food and place as:

> very obviously targeted at the audience's subliminal anxiety (fuelled by food scares, factory farming, superstore monopolies and other concerns) that food of obscure origin constitutes a potential threat. This anxiety can be temporarily relieved by embarking on a journey to an Arcadian sanctuary, which may be as easily located in Lancashire as in Belgium or in Morocco, where the confusing complexities of modern industrialised food chains have been reduced to a simple and transparent bilateral relationship between producer and consumer/cook.

Indeed, for a range of food programs, a sense of connection to one's food is often explicitly offered as an antidote to the alienation inherent to the modern food system.

Escape to River Cottage, which first aired in 1999, somewhat predated this 'mainstreaming' of food systems concerns. As the series progressed into the 2000s, however, it clearly spoke to the zeitgeist. By the time *Gourmet Farmer* launched in 2010, concerns about the perils of the modern food system had become well rehearsed; most 'foodie' audiences would have been at least somewhat familiar with these debates. Both *River Cottage* and *Gourmet Farmer* offer visions of 'emplaced' food existing largely outside the industrial food system.

As Hugh Fearnley-Whittingstall explains in the opening scene of *Escape to River Cottage*, his relocation from London to the Dorset countryside was motived by his "dream to escape the urban sprawl, find a little place in the country, and live off the fat of the land, thriving on whatever [he] can grow, gather or catch". Similarly, as the opening credits of *Gourmet Farmer* indicate, Matthew Evans's move from urban Sydney to rural Tasmania was propelled by his "dream ... of producing [his] own food, so [he] can know and trust what [he] eat[s]"—either by growing the food himself or being "no more than one degree of separation from the person who does". Both men's newfound access to food of known and 'trustworthy' origins is thus implicitly contrasted with the apparently anonymous and 'untrustworthy' food that characterised their previous urban existences. Thus, both *River Cottage* and *Gourmet Farmer* offer examples of food television's capacity to connect larger-scale concerns—such as a desire for an alternative to the industrial food system—to questions of individual lifestyle and "life politics" (Lewis 2012: 318, 319).

Beyond these basic premises, though, the shows tend to wear their politics lightly (Bonner 2011: 233). As Tania Lewis (2008b: 232) points out, the critical concerns of this type of culinary television tend to be presented in a less openly didactic manner than earlier modes of instructional cookery. But shows like *River Cottage* and *Gourmet Farmer* have nonetheless been interpreted as both political and pedagogical by scholars—including in my own previous work (Phillipov 2016, 2017). Specifically, these programs have typically been seen as an expression of the environmental and sustainability concerns that were gaining momentum around the same time (Bonner 2011: 231). For example, Parkins and Craig (2011: 191) describe the *River Cottage* series as marked by an ethical impulse towards more sustainable living, with Craig (2019: 144) more recently noting Fearnley-Whittingstall's "constant, focused attention on food politics across his programs". Others have read *River Cottage*'s self-sufficiency narrative as part of (or a precursor to) the green lifestyle or eco-reality TV genres, which seek to (re)imagine ways of reducing consumption and living within environmental limits (Bell & Hollows 2011; Lewis 2008b; Thomas 2008). *Gourmet Farmer* has been interpreted in similar terms (Lynch 2016).

Both programs have been read for their discourses of "alternative hedonism", in particular—through which the hosts seek both to avoid and to rectify the negative consequences of contemporary affluent consumption by seeking pleasure in different kinds of practices, specifically those that maintain an ethical, ecologically sustainable use of resources without requiring them to give up the "good life" (Soper

2004: 112, 2008: 571; Thomas 2008: 680–681). Alternative hedonism largely manifests in *River Cottage* and *Gourmet Farmer* as a rediscovery of the pleasures of sustainability, human connection, and slowness. For example, Fearnley-Whittingstall's newfound lifestyle gives him ample time to enjoy his animals and relax in his hammock, and even hard physical work (such as clearing and digging over a flowerbed to prepare it for sowing vegetables) is presented as "utterly rewarding and unalienated labour" (Bell & Hollows 2011: 182). For Evans, the time-consuming work of preserving gluts of fruit and vegetables is punctuated by plenty of time for relaxing and enjoying the fruits of his labours. When making passata to preserve the annual tomato harvest, for example, he seems to spend as much time enjoying lunch with friends as on the actual work of sauce-making. This focus on politics-as-pleasure, I have argued previously, is key to the shows' positive reframing of the work of sustainable consumption as enjoyable and politically progressive, rather than unpleasant drudgery (Phillipov 2016).

Such political interpretations have been assisted by both the broader media and cultural contexts of the time and the "paratexts" (Gray 2010) surrounding the shows' original broadcasts. In the case of the latter, the shows' accompanying cookbooks and websites contained more explicitly campaigning messages, which tended to offset, and served to contextualise, the relatively 'gentle' politics of the programs themselves (Bonner 2011: 234). Political interpretations of the *River Cottage* series were assisted, Frances Bonner (2011: 235) suggests, by its location on the UK's Channel 4—a network well-known for its campaigning food programs and whose website located Fearnley-Whittingstall's shows under the strapline "How to eat well, and ethically". The fact that most *River Cottage* scholarship emerged in the late 2000s and early 2010s has also contributed to scholars' tendency to read *River Cottage* on a continuum with Fearnley-Whittingstall's later "campaigning culinary documentaries", such as *Hugh's Chicken Run* (Bell & Hollows 2011). And, indeed, these later programs have provided lenses through which to 're-read' earlier *River Cottage* series. For instance, *River Cottage*'s pampered flock of layer hens has been reinterpreted by scholars as a political statement about animal welfare and environmental sustainability, when considered in the context of *Hugh's Chicken Run*—an explicitly political program designed to improve conditions of large-scale chicken and egg production, and which contrasts the idyllic lives of the River Cottage flock with the misery of battery chickens destined for the major supermarkets (Bell & Hollows 2011).

As Bonner (2011) argues, Fearnley-Whittingstall's own shift in focus has assisted (and, perhaps, necessitated) the interpretation of his earlier programs within an ethical and environmental frame:

> Over the years Fearnley-Whittingstall's programmes have moved from an initial, rather idiosyncratic, emphasis on improving his self-sufficiency in food ... to being able to be seen within a broader environmental frame. This has been a change not so much in his ambitions, as in the prevalence of green television programmes, which *enabled his to be seen in a more suitable context*.
> (Bonner 2011: 235, emphasis added)

From this perspective, critical engagement with *River Cottage*'s various texts and paratexts (e.g. *Hugh's Chicken Run*, the Channel 4 website, Fearnley-Whittingstall's books and cookbooks, the other 'green' television shows appearing around the same time) is thus vital to interpreting the politics of the show. A similar argument can be made in relation to *Gourmet Farmer*: Matthew Evans' campaigning culinary documentaries, politically inclined books and cookbooks, and public comment on food issues have provided a similarly "suitable context" for reading *Gourmet Farmer*'s politics.

The rural idyll and the politics of escape

Such attempts to read *River Cottage* and *Gourmet Farmer* in political terms, then, highlight the importance of historical and temporal contexts in accessing such meanings. However, once the texts move from broadcast television to streaming and catch-up services, they can become disengaged from the specificity of their original contexts. Stripped of their orienting contexts and paratexts, it is not clear that food television texts acquire the meanings that we have typically assumed. Indeed, it may be that their meanings need to be read anew when they appear in new contexts. This may especially be so for the circulation of food texts on platforms such as SBS On Demand, which not only disconnect programs from original broadcast contexts and paratexts (e.g. official websites, many of which are no longer available) but also offer viewers limited additional contextualising information (not even the shows' original broadcast or production date). While the shows' original broadcast contexts may have helped to direct particular interpretations, their *absence* potentially shapes different sorts of meanings. Of course, we cannot assume that historical contexts determine audience interpretations in any straightforward way, nor that audiences interpret texts in the same way as scholars. But the long-standing scholarly position that original contexts 'matter' has shaped a range of assumptions that may no longer hold about how environmental messaging manifests in television, and about the cultural salience and political power of such representations.

In the absence of a "suitable context" (Bonner 2011: 235) for interpreting the programs within an environmental frame, the narrative or flow prompted by catch-up TV seems just as likely to invite alternative readings. Indeed, the locations of *River Cottage* and *Gourmet Farmer* on the SBS On Demand platform provide a context for interpretation that may be less about environmental and sustainability concerns and more about the vicarious pleasures of "armchair travel" (Versteegen 2010: 459). Travel has long been a ubiquitous feature of food television (Strange 1998: 301). Even programs that do not necessarily suggest any travelling at all—such as Gordon Ramsay's *Kitchen Nightmares* or Jamie Oliver's *Naked Chef*—contain oblique references to travel (Versteegen 2010: 459). For example, one of the trademarks of *The Naked Chef* were the scenes of Oliver zipping about London on his Vespa to shop for ingredients, before taking the food home to cook for family and friends (Moseley 2001: 38; Versteegen 2010: 459). Scholars have, similarly, located *River Cottage* within the context of the food travelogue. Tania Lewis (2008b: 232), for example, describes it as part of the food tourism genre; she links the narratives of *River Cottage* to those of more explicitly travel-focused programming, such as *Jamie's Great Italian Escape* and Rick Stein's *Local Heroes*. For Lewis (2008b: 232), the travel motif serves as a vehicle for ethical concerns: a desire to protect and maintain 'authentic' and 'traditional' food practices in the face of modern food cultures dominated by industrialised convenience foods and globalised food practices.

River Cottage and *Gourmet Farmer* valorise traditional food practices through the hosts' use of pre-industrial methods of food production as signifiers of embeddedness and authenticity. Slow braising, home baking, preserving, hunting, and foraging all feature heavily, as do 'old-fashioned' dishes such as brawn. Meals are prepared without the assistance of modern appliances and kitchen equipment: wood-burning stoves and cast-iron pans replace stand mixers, food processors, and contemporary non-stick cookware (Phillipov 2016: 114). These traditional recipes and techniques are presented as helping to forge deeper connections between the hosts, their food, and their communities than was possible in their previous urban, supermarketised existences. For example, the traditional methods of preserving and charcuterie-making in which Evans and Fearnley-Whittingstall engage are presented as communal activities that simultaneously produce 'better' food than supermarket equivalents and connect the hosts with their friends and neighbours. That all this activity occurs in bucolic pastoral surrounds, featuring lush greenery, rolling hills, and story-book farmhouses, merely adds to the shows' utopian charms (see Thomas 2008: 686).

Lyn Thomas (2008: 691) argues that the pleasure of such programs resides in their reimagining of rural sustainability and self-sufficiency as avenues for a "free and stress-free life". This is perhaps more true of *River Cottage* than of *Gourmet Farmer*, where the financial and emotional challenges of farming (such as the death of livestock) are made much more explicit. But whatever the challenges the hosts face in their self-sufficiency experiments, their commitment to rural life never really results in serious hardship or struggle. Evans and Fearnley-Whittingstall are never tied to their land and instead have an almost utopian mobility, with a seemingly endless capacity to abandon their farms for fishing and hunting trips with friends, sorties to meet other producers, and opportunities to learn new skills. The travelogue components of both shows are key to their pedagogical and political impulses. It is through travel that the hosts learn, and teach others, about authentic food traditions—and, in the process, preserve and pass on traditional skills and ways of life threatened by industrial, globalised food systems.

I have previously argued that food television's "softly softly" approach to providing lessons in 'good' food consumption" (Lewis 2008b: 233) has been key to its political power, making political concerns with respect to food more appealing and more accessible to those who would not ordinarily identify with alternative political positions (Phillipov 2017). Yet this is also a double-edged sword. On the one hand, such an approach can invite viewers to reimagine political action as pleasurable and enjoyable—presenting sustainable lifestyles as a source of satisfaction, rather than deprivation. On the other hand, a "softly softly" politics does not tend to offer a clear 'preferred reading', thereby enabling other contexts and factors to shape the interpretation of textual meanings. The political ambiguity of these texts may be further amplified by the fact that their pleasures are primarily visual, rather than narrative: the visual pleasures of "close-ups of flowers, pastoral views, and interiors with wood-burning stoves, log fires, and heritage sinks, pots and pans and paintwork" (Thomas 2008: 690), not to mention the panoramic views of bucolic Dorset and Tasmanian landscapes. In the absence of a strong narrative invitation to interpret

Re-reading televisual flow 31

the shows' political significance in particular ways, readings may instead be shaped by other contexts.

And the contexts for interpretation provided by SBS On Demand are significantly different from those of their original broadcast airing. At the time of researching this chapter (early 2021), SBS Food was dominated by travel programming, with the majority of new acquisitions in this genre. On the platform's interface, which lists food programs alphabetically, *Gourmet Farmer* was positioned between *Gok Cooks Chinese* and *Hairy Bikers' Mississippi Adventure*. The *River Cottage* offering, *Tales from River Cottage*, appeared between *Sourced* (a show which, according to the program logline, sees host Guy Turland "eat his way around the planet") and *Taste the Nation with Padma Lakshmi* (a culinary tour of the US). These locations on the platform, along with the programs' own substantial travelogue components, may just as likely invite viewers to interpret *River Cottage* and *Gourmet Farmer* as part of the travel genre as to see them as eco-reality or green lifestyle TV. And if we are to interpret such texts as examples of armchair travel, it is not then clear why we should necessarily read them as expressing any kind of environmental or sustainability politics. This is not to suggest that the travel genre is incompatible with environmental or sustainability concerns; Lewis (2008a: 59, 2008b), for example, would argue that this is certainly not the case. Instead, it is to argue that the new forms of flow introduced by online delivery, alongside the shows' utopian impulses and "softly softly" politics, may invite viewers to see such programming as merely escapist entertainment, rather than reflecting a deeper investment in progressive political concerns. In this vein, Bonner (2011: 234)—who argued that the paratexts associated with the broadcast context were essential to the political interpretation of shows like *River Cottage*—views the travel genre as largely distinct from politically focused programming. She suggests that while such shows can and do advance ethical standpoints, they do so largely by subsuming their ethics into discourses of 'quality' and 'distinction'. Their promotion of 'fresh' and 'local' food, for example, "may be seen to involve green elements"—but their tendency to valorise rare breed meats, heritage vegetables, and free-range organic produce reveals their greater priority on demarcating and expressing class boundaries than bringing about change towards more sustainable ways of procuring, preparing, and eating food (Bonner 2011: 234).

Consequently, if the initial broadcasts of *River Cottage* and *Gourmet Farmer* could be seen as offering a 'gateway' to sustainable lifestyles—an alternative hedonist's reimagining of sustainability as a pleasure rather than a chore—this interpretation seems less likely once these programs move online. In the latter context, especially on a platform like SBS On Demand, there seems no particular reason why such texts should be seen to invite (let alone deliver audiences to) an environmental or sustainability politics. The shows' utopian impulses would seem just as likely to contribute to escapist fantasies of the rural idyll, or exclusionary practices of middle-class distinction, than an entry to a more progressive political position. Stripped of the "suitable context" (Bonner 2011: 235) for reading provided by their original broadcasts, we may be just as likely to interpret them through our present cultural lenses, rather than through those of their original time.

Meat and the climate crisis

From current perspectives, the notion that such texts should be read as parables of sustainability seems even more problematic. Indeed, there is something that looks profoundly *un*sustainable about Evans' and Fearnley-Whittingstall's so-called 'sustainable lifestyles' when considered from current environmental standpoints. In the years since the shows' original broadcasts, mainstream environmental discussion has shifted significantly from the broader (and somewhat vaguer) concept of 'sustainability' to a more explicit language of *climate crisis*. This has been accompanied by a shift in discourses about the kinds of social, cultural, and economic changes required to live in environmentally sustainable ways. Re-watching the shows in 2021, the lushness and green abundance of the landscapes—especially on *Gourmet Farmer*—seem almost shocking, considering the dryness and drought experienced elsewhere in Australia, and the devastating bushfires that ravaged much of the country in early 2020. Moreover, both shows' emphasis on meat consumption seems significantly out of step with contemporary environmental sensibilities. As already noted, the programs' narrative focus on raising livestock emerged at a time of significant concern about the health, environmental, and animal welfare consequences of industrial animal agriculture. Concerns about the nature of contemporary meat production were given prominence by Michael Pollan—who presented cattle feedlots as a key source of horror in *The Omnivore's Dilemma* (Pollan 2006)—and by Evans and Fearnley-Whittingstall in their campaigning culinary documentaries *For the Love of Meat* and *Hugh's Chicken Run*, which offered scathing critiques of industrial beef, chicken, and pork production in Australia and the UK. In contrast to the miserable lives of animals raised in large-scale, industrial conditions, the idyllic existences of Evans' and

Fearnley-Whittingstall's cows, chickens, and pigs—living in small family groups, free ranging in green pastures, and eating a 'natural' diet—were offered as an alternative, more ethical, model of meat production.

But read in our present context, in which animal agriculture has come into focus as a significant cause of climate change, the narrative emphasis on the raising of livestock (rather than, say, raising hardy native foods or drought-tolerant vegetable crops) now seems strangely anachronistic as an example of green lifestyle television. Even the hosts themselves have revised their earlier positions on meat consumption. Hugh Fearnley-Whittingstall, who had previously earned the nickname 'Hugh Fearlessly Eats it All' for his unapologetic carnivory (Fearnley-Whittingstall 2011a), now advocates significantly reducing meat consumption. His veg-centred cookbooks—*River Cottage: Veg Everyday!* (Fearnley-Whittingstall 2011b), *River Cottage: Much More Veg* (Fearnley-Whittingstall 2017), and *Eat Better Forever* (Fearnley-Whittingstall 2020)—encourage the uptake of plant-focused diets on health and sustainability grounds; *Eat Better Forever* outlines at some length the "disastrous" (Fearnley-Whittingstall 2020: 44) environmental and climate impacts of meat-heavy diets. In Evans' (2019) book, *On Eating Meat*, he advocates for eating less but better quality meat to ensure more sustainable environmental management of livestock production and higher welfare outcomes for food animals.

The message of 'less but better meat' is present in the original *River Cottage* and *Gourmet Farmer* television shows, but the philosophical and political underpinnings of this position largely reflected the 'ethical meat' debates taking place at the time (Arcari 2019; Pilgrim 2013)—the broader politics of which may not necessarily be visible to those unfamiliar with this earlier context. On *River Cottage* and *Gourmet Farmer*, both hosts' 'ethical' practices of livestock rearing are implicitly opposed to the 'unethical' activities of large agribusiness. But the problems of industrial farming are never explicitly addressed in either program: to do so would be to disrupt the easy pleasures of narratives focused on the bucolic lifestyle of the smallholder. Although both shows clearly demarcate their livestock animals *as food* in the shows' narratives—Evans even names his pigs "prosciutto" and "cassoulet"—they function almost as pets. In one episode, Fearnley-Whittingstall is shown sharing his porridge oats with his cows, and both hosts treat their pigs with the affection one might show a companion animal. "The dog gets jealous when I pat them", Evans says, as his pigs frolic in the sun. The effect is almost to reimagine the Australian and UK countrysides as places 'before' contemporary industrial animal agriculture—or as places where such practices simply do not exist. But with the horrors of the UK outbreaks of 'mad cow' disease likely to be fresh in the minds of British audiences at the time of *River Cottage*'s original release, and with health and animal welfare debates thoroughly mainstreamed by the time of *Gourmet Farmer*'s release over a decade later, most viewers would have been (at least peripherally) aware of the key issues to which the shows seek to present alternatives.

Consequently, the shows' representations of livestock production largely reflect the specificities of their cultural moments, in ways that may not be obvious to a present-day viewer. However, the insistent focus on meat consumption that now seems anachronistic as green lifestyle television may perhaps seem less out of place if the shows are instead understood as escapist travelogues. Seen from this perspective, Evans' and Fearnley-Whittingstall's green pastures, filled with pampered livestock, can be seen to activate a nostalgia for rural life, reflecting long-standing urban romanticisation of the country (Bell 2006; Burchardt 2002; Williams 1973). Such programs can thus be seen as offering an essentially urban conception of the rural, in which the countryside is an (imagined) panacea to the problems of city life. As a result, these programs can simply provide the audience with pleasurable fantasies as remote from their everyday lives as the "Arcadian sanctuar[ies]" of the Belgian or Moroccan travelogues (Versteegen 2010: 459) they appear alongside—without any necessary evidence of deeper political, environmental, or sustainability imperatives.

Rethinking digital flow

The likelihood that these programs will be interpreted as examples of green lifestyle television is further diminished by the "planned flow" during the programs themselves. As a free service, SBS supports its online platform primarily through advertising. SBS On Demand features less advertising than free-to-air broadcasts, but the advertising that does appear is especially repetitive, with the same ads often appearing in every ad break, and sometimes multiple times in the *same* ad break—a common source of complaint for viewers (Christiansen 2015). If, as Raymond Williams (1973 [2003]: 91) argued, the "real flow" is not the "published sequence of programme items but this sequence transformed by the inclusion of another kind of sequence" (i.e. the insertion of advertising), then the combination of advertising and program content that produces the televisual 'flow' in the online context works to construct additional narratives that can guide the interpretation of texts. When re-watching the programs in early 2021, advertising breaks for *River Cottage* and *Gourmet Farmer* were dominated by George Clooney's ad for Nespresso coffee, a product with a hefty environmental footprint (Gunther 2015), and Nigella Lawson's ad for Whittaker's chocolate, a product with its own sustainability concerns (Schreiber 2020).

Given the extent to which the meanings in the advertising breaks can rub off onto the shows' meanings (Gray & Lotz 2012: 127), the relentless advertising for products with questionable sustainability credentials would seem to complicate these shows' capacities to imagine the alternatives to overconsumption that scholars have understood as a key feature of green lifestyle television (Lewis 2012: 318). In other words, the capacity of green lifestyle television to foreground notions of green citizenship, through its articulation of the "growing relationship between large-scale global environmental concerns and questions of lifestyle" (Lewis 2012: 319), would seem to be complicated by repetitive messages to engage in more and unsustainable consumption—not just of products featured in the ad breaks, but also products (such as meat) featured within the program narratives. Combined, these would seem to diminish the invitation to read the shows in the political terms that have been a key framework for scholarly understanding of their meaning and significance.

I have previously argued that food television's politics-as-pleasure has been key to mainstreaming its political messages (Phillipov 2017). By this logic, food television can serve as a gateway to alternative forms and experiences of consumption—expanding the "politics of the possible" (Guthman 2008: 1181) by offering us alternative visions of what it might mean to consume more responsibly and sustainably, and to see these changes as sources of pleasure rather than deprivation. But once removed from the linear television schedule and shifted into the online database, such food programs may no longer realise their full progressive potential. In the expanded and perpetual present of digital media (Coleman 2018), whereby the shows are removed from their "suitable context" (Bonner 2011: 235) for interpretation, food television's representations of pleasurable lifestyles can become more closely linked to escapist travel programming or messages promoting unsustainable consumption than broader sustainability or environmental concerns.

It is perhaps telling that while Evans' and Fearnley-Whittingstall's campaigning culinary documentaries have also appeared on SBS On Demand, they have not typically appeared in the 'Food' section. For example, *What's the Catch?*, *Hugh's Fat Fight*, and *Hugh's War on Waste* all appeared in the 'Documentaries' section of the platform. The decision to exclude more hard-hitting programming from the Food section was likely taken so as to not disrupt this section's emphasis on easy-going pleasures, but it also serves to evacuate both shows from the broader contexts that might have encouraged *River Cottage* and *Gourmet Farmer* to be understood in more explicitly political terms (and previously assisted in doing so). In short, *River Cottage* and *Gourmet Farmer* are examples of shows that were previously interpreted as political, but whose content can be readily redirected to serve a broader consumerist menu, in which the "alternative hedonist" may simply be left with the "hedonism" without the "alternative". This highlights the necessity of developing strategies for reorienting both our politics and our critical approaches to better capture the current contexts in which food television is circulated and produced. As the next chapter will show, it may be that the politics of food television, increasingly, is no longer about food at all, but about other aspects of our social and economic lives—and this, too, must be reflected in our critiques.

References

Arcari, Paula 2019, 'The ethical masquerade: (Un)masking mechanisms of power behind "ethical" meat'. In Michelle Phillipov & Katherine Kirkwood (eds), *Alternative Food Politics: From the Margins to the Mainstream*. Routledge: London, pp. 169–189.

Ashley, Bob, Hollows, Joanne, Jones, Steve & Taylor, Ben 2004, *Food and Cultural Studies*. Routledge: London.

Bell, David 2006, 'Variations on the rural idyll'. In Paul Cloke, Terry Marsden & Patrick Mooney (eds), *Handbook of Rural Studies*. Sage: London, pp. 149–160.

Bell, David & Hollows, Joanne 2011, 'From *River Cottage* to *Chicken Run*: Hugh Fearnley-Whittingstall and the class politics of ethical consumption', *Celebrity Studies*, vol. 2, no. 2, pp. 178–191. https://doi.org/10.1080/19392397.2011.574861

Bellanova, Rocco & González Fuster, Gloria 2018, 'No (big) data, no fiction? Thinking surveillance with/against Netflix'. In Ann Rudinow Sætnan, Ingrid Schneider & Nicola Green (eds), *The Politics and Policies of Big Data: Big Data Big Brother?* Routledge: London, pp. 227–246.

Bonner, Frances 2011, 'Lifestyle television: Gardening and the good life'. In Tania Lewis & Emily Potter (eds), *Ethical Consumption: A Critical Introduction*. Routledge: London, pp. 231–242.

Burchardt, Jeremy 2002, *Paradise Lost: Rural Idyll and Social Change Since 1800*. I.B. Tauris: London.

Campbell, Hugh 2009, 'Breaking new ground in food regime theory: Corporate environmentalism, ecological feedbacks and the "food from

Re-reading televisual flow 37

somewhere" regime?' *Agriculture and Human Values*, vol. 26, no. 4, pp. 309–319. https://doi.org/10.1007/s10460-009-9215-8

Christiansen, Nic 2015, 'Viewers bemoan amount of ads on catch up TV services but like fact they are free, finds study', *Mumbrella*, 10 December, https://mumbrella.com.au/viewers-bemoan-amount-of-ads-on-catch-up-tv-services-but-like-fact-they-are-free-finds-study-334688. Accessed 14 January 2022.

Coleman, Rebecca 2018, 'Theorizing the present: Digital media, pre-emergence and infra-structures of feeling', *Cultural Studies*, vol. 32, no. 4, pp. 600–622. https://doi.org/10.1080/09502386.2017.1413121

Cox, Christopher M. 2018, 'Programming—Flow in the convergence of digital media platforms and television', *Critical Studies in Television: The International Journal of Television Studies*, vol. 13, no. 4, pp. 438–454. https://doi.org/10.1177/1749602018796681

Craig, Geoffrey 2019, *Media, Sustainability and Everyday Life*. Palgrave Macmillan: London.

Curtin, Michael 2009, 'Matrix Media'. In Graeme Turner & Ginna Tay (eds), *Television Studies After TV: Understanding Television in the Post-Broadcast Era*. Routledge: London & New York, pp. 9–19.

de Solier, Isabelle 2008, 'Foodie makeovers: Public service television and lifestyle guidance'. In Gareth Palmer (ed.), *Exposing Lifestyle Television: The Big Reveal*. Ashgate: Aldershot, pp. 65–81.

Evans, Matthew 2019, *On Eating Meat*. Murdoch Books: Crows Nest, NSW.

Fearnley-Whittingstall, Hugh 2011a, *Hugh Fearlessly Eats It All: Dispatches from the Gastronomic Front Line*. Bloomsbury: London.

Fearnley-Whittingstall, Hugh 2011b, *River Cottage: Veg Everyday!* Bloomsbury: London.

Fearnley-Whittingstall, Hugh 2017, *River Cottage: Much More Veg*. Bloomsbury: London.

Fearnley-Whittingstall, Hugh 2020, *Eat Better Forever*. Bloomsbury: London.

Gilbert, Anne 2019, 'Push, pull, rerun: Television reruns and streaming media', *Television & New Media*, vol. 20, no. 7, pp. 686–701. https://doi.org/10.1177/1527476419842418

Goodman, David 2003. 'The quality "turn" and alternative food practices: Reflections and agenda', *Journal of Rural Studies*, vol. 19, no. 1, pp. 1–7. https://doi.org/10.1016/S0743-0167(02)00043-8

Gray, Jonathan 2010, *Show Sold Separately: Promos, Spoilers, and Other Media Paratexts*. New York University Press: New York.

Gray, Jonathan & Lotz, Amanda D. 2012, *Television Studies*. Polity: Cambridge.

Gunther, Marc 2015, 'The good, the bad and the ugly: Sustainability at Nespresso', *The Guardian*, 28 May, https://www.theguardian.com/sustainable-business/2015/may/27/nespresso-sustainability-transparency-recycling-coffee-pods-values-aluminum. Accessed 14 January 2022.

Guthman, Julie 2008, 'Neoliberalism and the making of food politics in California', *Geoforum*, vol. 39, no. 3, pp. 1171–1183. https://doi.org/10.1016/j.geoforum.2006.09.002

Hinrichs, C. Clare 2003, 'The practices and politics of food system localization', *Journal of Rural Studies*, vol. 19, no. 1, pp. 33–45. https://doi.org/10.1016/S0743-0167(02)00040-2

Hoyt, Eric 2014, *Hollywood Vault: Film Libraries before Home Video*. University of California Press: Berkeley.

Jenner, Mareike 2016, 'Is this TVIV? On Netflix, TVIII and binge-watching', *New Media & Society*, vol. 18, no. 2, pp. 257–273. https://doi.org/10.1177/1461444814541523

Kompare, Derek 2005, *Rerun Nation: How Repeats Invented American Television*. Routledge: New York.

Kompare, Derek 2010, 'Reruns 2.0: Revising repetition for multiplatform television distribution', *Journal of Popular Film and Television*, vol. 38, no. 2, pp. 79–83. https://doi.org/10.1080/01956051.2010.483353

Lewis, Tania 2008a, *Smart Living: Lifestyle Media and Popular Expertise*. Peter Lang: New York.

Lewis, Tania 2008b, 'Transforming citizens? Green politics and ethical consumption on lifestyle television', *Continuum: Journal of Media & Cultural Studies*, vol. 22, no. 2, pp. 227–240. https://doi.org/10.1080/10304310701864394

Lewis, Tania 2012, '"There grows the neighbourhood": Green citizenship, creativity and life politics on eco-TV', *International Journal of Cultural Studies*, vol. 15, no. 3, pp. 315–326. https://doi.org/10.1177/1367877911433753

Littler, Jo 2008, *Radical Consumption: Shopping for Change in Contemporary Culture*. Open University Press: Maidenhead.

Lobato, Ramon 2018, 'Rethinking international TV flows research in the age of Netflix', *Television & New Media*, vol. 19, no. 3, pp. 241–256. https://doi.org/10.1177/1527476417708245

Lynch, Bernardine 2016, 'Australian culinary television: Visions of the real', *MEDIANZ*, vol. 16, no. 2. https://doi.org/10.11157/medianz-vol16iss2id208.

Manovich, Lev 2002, *The Language of New Media*. The MIT Press: Cambridge.

Miller, Toby 2007, *Cultural Citizenship: Cosmopolitanism, Consumerism and Television in a Neoliberal Age*. Temple University Press: Philadelphia, PA.

Moseley, Rachel 2001, '"Real lads do cook….but some things are still hard to talk about": The gendering of 8–9', *European Journal of Cultural Studies*, vol. 4, no. 1, pp. 32–39. https://doi.org/10.1177/136754940100400102

Nelan, Bruce, Jansson, Edward & Szabo, Lisa 2017, 'An overview of farmers markets in Australia'. In Judy A. Harrison (ed.), *Food Safety for Farmers Markets: A Guide to Enhancing Safety of Local Foods*. Springer: Cham, pp. 103–117.

Newbury, Michael 2012, 'Fast zombie/slow zombie: Food writing, horror movies, and agribusiness apocalypse', *American Literary History*, vol. 24, no. 1, pp. 87–114. https://doi.org/10.1093/alh/ajr055

Parkins, Wendy & Craig, Geoffrey 2011, 'Slow living and the temporalities of sustainable consumption'. In Tania Lewis & Emily Potter (eds), *Ethical Consumption: A Critical Introduction*. Routledge: London, pp. 189–210.

Phillipov, Michelle 2016, 'Escaping to the country: Media, nostalgia, and the new food industries', *Popular Communication*, vol. 14, no. 2, pp. 111–122. https://doi.org/10.1080/15405702.2015.1084620

Phillipov, Michelle 2017, *Media and Food Industries: The New Politics of Food*. Palgrave Macmillan: Cham.

Phillipov, Michelle 2019, 'Thinking with Media: Margins, Mainstreams and the Media Politics of Food'. In Michelle Phillipov & Katherine Kirkwood (eds), *Alternative Food Politics: From the Margins to the Mainstream*. Routledge: London, pp. 1–19.

Pilgrim, Karyn 2013, '"Happy cows," "happy beef": A critique of the rationales for ethical meat', *Environmental Humanities*, vol. 3, no. 1, pp. 111–127. https://doi.org/10.1215/22011919-3611257

Pollan, Michael 2006, *The Omnivore's Dilemma: A Natural History of Four Meals*. Penguin: London.

Pollan, Michael 2008, *In Defence of Food*. Penguin: London.

SBS 2013, *Annual Report 2012–2013*, http://media.sbs.com.au/home/upload_media/site_20_rand_602172661_sbs_annual_report_2011_12.pdf. Accessed 14 July 2021.

SBS 2015, 'SBS dishes up Australia's first free channel for everyday food lovers' (Media Release), 30 September, https://media.sbs.com.au/home/upload_media/site_20_rand_603839014_media_release_sbs_dishes_up_australias_first_free_channel_for_everyday_food_lovers.pdf. Accessed 14 July 2021.

SBS 2020a, *Annual Report 2019–2020*, https://www.sbs.com.au/aboutus/sites/sbs.com.au.aboutus/files/sbs_annual_report_2019-20_final.pdf. Accessed 14 July 2021.

SBS 2020b, 'SBS Charter', https://www.sbs.com.au/aboutus/sbs-charter. Accessed 14 July 2021.

Schlosser, Eric 2002, *Fast Food Nation: What the All-American Meal is Doing to the World*. Penguin: London.

Schreiber, Melody 2020, 'The challenge of sustainable chocolate', *The New Republic*, 14 February, https://newrepublic.com/article/156569/challenge-sustainable-chocolate. Accessed 14 January 2022.

Soper, Kate 2004, 'Rethinking the "good life": The consumer as citizen', *Capitalism Nature Socialism*, vol. 15, no. 3, pp. 111–116. https://doi.org/10.1080/1045575042000247293

Soper, Kate 2008, 'Alternative hedonism, cultural theory and the role of aesthetic revisioning', *Cultural Studies*, vol. 22, no. 5, pp. 567–587. https://doi.org/10.1080/09502380802245829

Strange, Niki 1998, 'Perform, educate, entertain: Ingredients of the cookery programme genre'. In Christine Geraghty & David Lusted (eds), *The Television Studies Book*. London: Arnold, pp. 301–312.

Thomas, Lyn 2008, 'Alternative realities: Downshifting narratives in contemporary lifestyle television', *Cultural Studies*, vol. 22, no. 5, pp. 680–699. https://doi.org/10.1080/09502380802245936

Versteegen, Heinrich 2010, 'Armchair epicures: The proliferation of food programmes on British TV'. In Marion Gymnich & Norbert Lennartz (eds), *The Pleasures and Horrors of Eating: The Cultural History of Eating in Anglophone Literature*. V&R Unipress: Göttingen, pp. 447–464.

Warsaw, Phillip, Archambault, Steven, He, Arden & Miller, Stacy 2021, 'The economic, social, and environmental impacts of farmers markets: Recent evidence from the US', *Sustainability*, vol. 13, no. 6. https://doi.org/10.3390/su13063423

Williams, Raymond 1973, *The Country and the City*. Oxford University Press: Oxford.

Williams, Raymond 1974 [2003], *Television: Technology and Cultural Form*. Routledge: London.

2 Streaming reality
Neoliberal subjectivities, aspirational labour, and Netflix food programming

As Chapter 1 has shown, digital distribution has disrupted established scholarly understandings of the politics of 'older' food television texts, including how and where this politics occurs. This chapter turns to changes associated with digital-first food content, particularly that of streaming services. The chapter focuses on Netflix, given its significant investments in originally produced content in recent years and its outpacing of competitors in both quantity and quality of food programming. Netflix food programs have generated consistently glowing accounts from media and industry, comparing the platform's offerings favourably with the apparently stale food fare on broadcast and cable networks. *The Guardian*, for example, has declared that Netflix has "revolutionised" food TV, replacing network television's "recycled outputs, flabby formats and [uninspired] talent rosters" with "credible international talent and creative shows that demand a binge" (Brearley 2018). In *The New Yorker*, Kyle Chayka (2020) described Netflix food shows as a form of "ambient TV": soothing, frictionless viewing in which seductive visual pleasures are prioritised over factual content or narrative involvement.

Others have emphasised the distinctly comforting, uplifting quality of Netflix food programming, especially when compared with network TV. Writing for *Fast Company*, Cale Guthrie Weissman (2019) offers a typical example, characterising Netflix food programming as:

> warm, sun-kissed, and generally uplifting, without ever stooping to cheap pathos. Netflix has yet to produce a cynical *Cutthroat Kitchen*-style program, or the "I need the $10,000 prize to achieve my very small dream" formula that helped spoil *Chopped*. It can't be overstated how *Nailed It!* never devolves into the sneering of *Worst Cooks in America*. The streamer's brand of food TV might as well be called Comfort Me With Netflix.

DOI: 10.4324/9781003261940-3

42 *Streaming reality*

This association of Netflix food shows with *comfort* is especially interesting given that Netflix's primary area of growth has been in competition reality programs—including *Sugar Rush, Nailed It!, Crazy Delicious, Best Leftovers Ever!,* and *Cooked with Cannabis,* among others. Quirky and light-hearted many of these programs may be, but describing them as "comforting" seems a rather unusual characterisation of competition-based food TV—and one that would seem to confound many of our usual scholarly assumptions about what such programs mean and how the politics of food-focused reality TV are typically mobilised.

In order to examine in more detail this seemingly perplexing shift in the meanings of digital food TV, this chapter considers two recent Netflix Original programs, *Crazy Delicious* and *Sugar Rush.* Each draws elements from earlier broadcast and cable reality gameshows, but relocates them in the new industry contexts, audience practices, and algorithmic logics of streaming television. *Crazy Delicious,* a co-production between Netflix and the UK's Channel 4, is a cooking competition in which each episode sees three "inventive home cooks" compete over three rounds. Hosted by British comedian Jayde Adams, the show is set in a whimsical Garden of Eden, in which contestants must forage for ingredients in a "magical edible garden" filled with edible statues, a Prosecco waterfall, and fruits and vegetables ripe for the picking. They are watched and judged by "food gods" Carla Hall, Heston Blumenthal, and Niklas Ekstedt, who (dressed all in white) preside over the contestants in a heaven-themed mezzanine. *Crazy Delicious* first aired on UK Channel 4 in January 2020, before being released on Netflix in June. With nods to popular UK shows like *The Great British Bake Off,* an international cast of judges, and contestants from across the Atlantic, the show was designed for simultaneous appeal to British and international audiences. *Crazy Delicious* currently appears in 35 Netflix regions, including nine of Netflix's ten largest markets.[1]

Sugar Rush is a Netflix Original production first aired in 2018. Each episode features four teams of professional bakers, making cupcakes, confections, and cakes to vie for a $10,000 cash prize. Hosted by YouTube celebrity Holden March, and judged by American pastry chef and entrepreneur Candace Nelson and Australian *pâtissier* Adriano Zumbo, *Sugar Rush* is now in its third season (or its fifth, counting its two Christmas spin-offs). It appears in 36 Netflix regions, including Netflix's ten largest markets. Unlike *Crazy Delicious,* whose program conventions originate from broadcast television, *Sugar Rush* draws its inspiration more directly from the Food Network, sharing a similar format to *Cake Wars* and *Cupcake Wars,* with some crossover of personnel (for example, Nelson was also a judge on *Cupcake Wars*). But *Sugar Rush*'s shorter, compact seasons and its more star-studded, international cast (including an Australian judge and a revolving array of guest judges drawn from the Netflix stable of actors and comedians) have moved the show beyond the Food Network's traditional market niche, with a more international mode of address.

The confluence of textual representations, production practices, and platform infrastructures characterising both programs offers a productive 'way in' for analysing the textual, ideological, and affective functioning of these newer forms of reality TV. What is revealed, I argue, is a new politics of food TV that necessitates thinking 'beyond' food to better understand the cultural place of food television texts, the digital platforms that house them, and their broader social and economic contexts. The chapter begins by contrasting *Crazy Delicious* and *Sugar Rush* with earlier forms of broadcast and cable reality TV. Many of the combative, disciplinary, and pedagogical functions that we have come to expect of reality programming are significantly diminished within these newer programs' narratives, which focus on feel-good pleasures and adopt conventions drawn from what Jorie Lagerwey (2018) calls the "loving reality" genre of reality TV. However, while both shows certainly exhibit a range of features consistent with loving reality, I argue that Netflix food programs merely *appear* to be "loving" and easy-going. This is because, rather than dramatising the production of neoliberal subjectivities, as in classic examples of reality TV (Hearn 2014; Ouellette & Hay 2008a; Palmer 2004), Netflix food competitions typically *begin* with the fully formed neoliberal subject as their starting point. In doing so, such programs persistently reframe contestants' labour as *leisure*, in ways that allow the streaming service to profit from pre-existing identities, brands, and content, much as its algorithmic logics extract value from the digital labour of audiences. This, in turn, highlights the contribution of contemporary food programming to significantly expanding the types of unpaid "aspirational labour" (Duffy 2017) that have become normalised and taken-for-granted in contemporary media—and in which the invisibilisation of work on screen increasingly mirrors the invisibilisation of work in Netflix's own platform logic and in digital capitalism more generally.

Reality television and neoliberal pedagogy

Although Netflix competition shows like *Crazy Delicious* and *Sugar Rush* share conventions with earlier forms of broadcast and cable reality television, they also, in some quite significant ways, disrupt dominant understandings of these genres. Reality TV emerged at a specific historical moment, when the "reinvention of television" following the industry's economic woes of the 1990s and 2000s converged with the Anglo-American "reinvention of government" in the late 20th century (Ouellette & Hay 2008a: 2). This has significantly shaped scholarly understandings of what reality TV 'means' as a television genre. On an industrial level, reality television has been analysed as an early adopter of production practices that embrace the flexible, precarious working conditions of post-Fordist capitalism (Hearn 2008a, 2014; Ross 2014). On a textual level, it has been understood as an "instructional template ... [for] empowered citizenship" in a neoliberal era (Ouellette & Hay 2008a: 17; see also Lewis 2008; Miller 2007).

Reality television has not only contributed to significant savings in production costs by eliminating the need for expensive actors and writers, necessary for scripted programming (Hearn 2008a, 2014; Ross 2014). It has also resulted in the production of genres—from cooking competitions to housing makeovers to weight loss programs— that focus on aspects of everyday life as sites of self-improvement (Bell & Hollows 2005; Bonner 2003; Lewis 2008). From *Idol* to *The Biggest Loser*, reality television has been understood as the "quintessential technology of citizenship of our age" (Ouellette & Hay 2008b: 472). In much of the scholarship on reality television, its pedagogical impulses—including its reframing of personal and domestic management as sites of both pleasure and responsibility (Lewis 2008: 13)— have been read as an inevitable end point of neoliberal governance. From this perspective, reality television's life interventions "enact the reasoning that people who are floundering can and must be taught to develop and maximize their capacities for normalcy, happiness, material stability, and success rather than rely on a public 'safety net'" (Ouellette & Hay 2008b: 476; see also Ouellette & Hay 2008a: 67).

In other words, if neoliberalism represents the "extension and installation of competitive markets into all areas of life" (Birch 2015: 572), reality television is understood as explicitly narrating the behaviours and presentational forms best suited to the current moment in capitalism (Moseley 2001: 34; Ouellette & Hay 2008a). This includes the adoption of neoliberal values such as self-responsibility, self-help, and self-performance (Johanssen 2017: 198) and a conception of the self as an "enterprise ... to be invested in" (Palmer 2004: 185). On a reality makeover show, this might involve equipping contestants with a new wardrobe or a new diet to produce a happier, healthier, more productive version of themselves. On a reality cooking competition program, this might be presented as an ideology of merit, in which contestants put their heart and soul into their work for a chance to realise their food 'dream'. In ignoring or diminishing structural barriers to success, the capacity to achieve one's 'dream' is often presented as universal and classless. But reality television's typical notions of 'good' citizenship—including its ideas about what constitutes 'good' food, 'good' housekeeping, or a 'good' life—are frequently critiqued for their adoption of middle-class modes of living that position working-class participants as socially deficient and in need of reform (Lewis 2008; Palmer 2004; Skeggs & Wood 2011).

Reality television, then, has been understood to dramatise and reward the types of subjectivities required to succeed in neoliberal capitalism. Contestants are frequently disciplined through surveillance techniques—including scathing critiques, hidden cameras, high-pressure scenarios, and other methods of shaming and humiliation—through which 'bad' choices (of dress, diet, lifestyle) can be 'corrected' and transformed (Palmer 2004; Wood & Skeggs 2011). Such techniques are especially prominent in the makeover show, but they are also a feature of the reality competition show, where winning is framed as 'transformative' and 'life-changing'. This is narrativised especially clearly via the phenomenon of the reality 'journey', framed in the language of 'learning' and 'growth' (Seale 2012) and aimed at the production of a marketable self-brand that can be capitalised on at the conclusion of the competition (Hearn 2014).

Success on a broadcast reality show like *MasterChef*, for example, relies on contestants' ability to "put [themselves] on a plate" (Lewis 2011) and produce an increasingly finessed personal brand that can be translated into a new food career, new media roles, and/or new celebrity status at the conclusion of filming. Many contestants deploy their ethnic and cultural heritage as a foundation of their unique food 'brand': the homely 'Aussie mum' persona of Australia's season 1 winner, Julie Goodwin, was just as key to her broad appeal as the hybrid European-Asian identity of season 2 winner Adam Liaw (Lewis 2011). But reality cooking competitions are not just about feel-good personal brands, nor are they completely free of the humiliation and shaming that typifies the makeover genre. Tasha Oren (2013: 30) identifies conflict, humiliation, and failure as key elements of the reality cooking contest:

> In these top-rated competition formats, chefs race around in utter panic to complete each 'challenge' under strict time limits, are subjected to harsh criticism or degrading dress-down by a panel

of judges, and then, one by one, are dismissed with a gravely intoned catch-phrase ('Pack up your knives and go', 'You have been chopped', or 'Take off your jacket and leave the kitchen'). Competition shows trade on displacement, confusion and discomfort as important pre-conditions to productivity. As much as beautiful dishes, skilfully made, they also offer stress, discord and reproach.

Success on reality competitions, then, can be understood as dramatising both the risk and the entrepreneurial subjectivities that have become increasingly naturalised components of life under neoliberal capitalism. These include the intensification of work and the precarity of the labour market that have necessitated the blurring of work and personal identities and the ongoing maintenance of marketable self-brands (Boltanski & Chiapello 2005). In the context of reality television, self-branding can be understood as a distinct kind of labour—though not one remunerated by traditional means, since reality contestants are typically paid little more than travel costs and a per diem.

For the majority of contestants on traditional reality TV, the reward for appearing on the show is primarily the opportunity to be 'fixed' or transformed (in the makeover genre) or to be in the running to receive a potentially life-changing prize (in the competition show). For especially successful participants, newfound celebrity may await them at the conclusion of the show. Indeed, it has been widely acknowledged that celebrity is one of the key sites of value for the reality television industry (Redden 2018: 411)—so much so that producers and networks generally consider contestants' prospects of free self-promotion to be an adequate form of compensation for their involvement (Ross 2014: 35). Typically, this means that participants' work is not recognised as work at all: instead, producers and networks "position themselves as benign corporate benefactors [assisting participants to improve their lives] and the participants as their grateful beneficiaries" (Hearn 2008a: 503). In these respects, the work of reality television can thus be seen to reflect what has variously been termed "aspirational labour" (Duffy 2017), "hope labour" (Kuehn & Corrigan 2013), and "venture labour" (Neff 2012), whereby un- or underpaid work is undertaken in the present in the hope of further work or compensation in the future.

Like the *Idol* or *Top Model* contestant progressively mastering image-management techniques over the course of a season, reality television often "explicitly narrate[s] the hard work involved in becoming a celebrity brand" (Hearn 2014: 444). Given that the personas and presentational forms of celebrity are now increasingly adopted within the self-branding routines of ordinary people, reality celebrities (it has been argued) model many of the effective performance, communicative, and image skills required for the production of the entrepreneurial branded self under contemporary capitalism (Bennett & Holmes 2010: 66; Hearn 2008b: 207). This notion of reality TV as fundamentally pedagogical—where contestants and (in turn) audiences are instructed in navigating the contemporary conditions of post-Fordist capitalism—has significantly shaped several decades of scholarship on what reality TV is and how it works, both textually and ideologically.

"Loving reality"

On the surface, Netflix Original cooking competitions would seem to resist many of these conventional scholarly understandings. In fact, despite some shared lineages, many Netflix food programs appear to be about as far away as possible from the broadcast and cable reality competition fare that has been the subject of most academic scholarship to date. Netflix reality competitions appear to leave little space for the journeys of personal or professional transformation, the conflict and competitive individualism, and the production of celebrity that typify network reality TV. The fact that most programs feature new contestants in each episode disrupts the season-long reality 'journeys' essential for crowning the next singing star, master chef, or weight loss success. On *Crazy Delicious* and *Sugar Rush*, the viewer is offered a brief back-story for each contestant, but nothing in detail, and the shows' narrative and episodic structures are not designed to reveal change or transformation over time.

The shows are also refreshingly free of the drama and conflict that typify earlier forms of reality TV: the relentless disciplining of contestants and exhortations to give the competition one's 'all' are pleasantly absent from most Netflix food programs. While some contestants do appear visibly stressed while undertaking challenges, and failures are sometimes evident, there are no dramatic meltdowns. In contrast to traditional reality cooking competitions like *MasterChef* and *My Kitchen Rules*, where contestants live away from their families for weeks on end and compete while suffering from sleep deprivation, long days, and early mornings, the competition structures of *Crazy Delicious* and *Sugar Rush* are far gentler to contestants, minimising the potential for emotional outbursts and other forms of conflict. On *My Kitchen Rules*, for example, contestants must submit numerous menu options in advance of challenges, only to be told the night before which they will be cooking, preventing them from practising their chosen dishes (or, sometimes, even familiarising themselves with them) and thereby increasing the potential for drama and disaster. In contrast, *Crazy Delicious* not only gives contestants enough notice that they can practise dishes in advance, it also permits them to bring some pre-prepared items from home, such as specialised ingredients or home-made decorations. On *Sugar Rush*, contestants undertake baking challenges under time pressure, but time limits are realistic, and contestants are able to bank unused time from earlier rounds, creating fewer conditions for tears and meltdowns.

One of the key drivers of reality TV, for both audiences and advertisers, is often understood to be its excess of affect (Bonner 2005; Kavka 2014). This is an especially obvious feature of the makeover genre, variously characterised by humiliation, shaming, embarrassing intimate details, and spectacular bodily horrors (Johanssen 2017). But it is also a product of the competition show, where an ethos of "putting everything on the line" and "winner takes all" produces an affective surplus. As Oren observes, there is an intense corporeality to the reality cooking contest: popular food television is a "tense and sweaty affair, featuring … impossible assignments, rushed preparations, costly mistakes, and withering assessments" (Oren 2013: 23). Some broadcast programs, such as *MasterChef*, have side-stepped the worst excesses of the competition format through family-friendly and congenial representations of ethnic and class diversity (Lewis 2011). But the "awkward materialities" (Kavka 2014: 462) of contestants' cooking disasters, tears, and meltdowns have nonetheless been central to the narrative and advertising tropes of even these more 'feel good' programs, with such events receiving pride of place in interstitial spot advertising and pre-ad-break cliff-hangers. Indeed, the affective charge of such moments has often been a key mechanism through which reality television compels viewers to watch in the broadcast schedule, engage in watercooler culture, and participate in social media discussion during and after episode broadcasts (Ashley et al. 2004: 174).

Netflix cooking competitions, in contrast, typically offer a dampening down of intensity in favour of even more easy-going viewing pleasures. With no prizes on *Crazy Delicious* (merely a symbolic "golden apple") and only a modest $10,000 prize for winners of *Sugar Rush*, competition outcomes are relatively low stakes. Even on *Sugar Rush*, the cash prize is rarely presented as a strong motivator for entering. Camaraderie, rather than competition, is emphasised, with contestants frequently congratulating each other and offering words of encouragement. Judging is much gentler and more collegial than we have come to expect of competition programming. Judges on both *Crazy Delicious* and *Sugar Rush* typically emphasise the positive aspects of dishes, even in cases of failure, and judges on *Crazy Delicious*, in particular, are always careful to thank contestants warmly for their efforts, whether or not a dish has been a success.

The easy-going nature of both shows is further reinforced by their carefully constructed diversity, with contestants drawn from a range of age groups and ethnic, class, gender, and sexual identities. Such harmonious representations of difference depart from the normalising and pathologising impulses of many earlier reality TV programs, particularly those targeting working class participants (Johanssen 2017; Ouellette & Hay 2008a), and put *Crazy Delicious* and *Sugar Rush* more on a continuum with shows like *MasterChef* and *The Great British Bake Off* with their diverse multicultural casts (see Lagerwey 2018; Lewis 2011). Both programs' cheerful, almost camp, sensibilities further add to their upbeat tone. *Crazy Delicious* host Jayde Adams works to lighten the mood through flirtatious interactions with the judges and slapstick food gags (such as biting into an array of edible food sculptures, from cherubs to watering cans)—as do the various guest judges on *Sugar Rush*, including comedians, actors, and other celebrities. The appearance of different body types, including plus-sized women enjoying food with gusto (such as Adams on *Crazy Delicious* and comedians like Fortune Feimster on *Sugar Rush*), serves to foreground the pleasures of food and cooking without the moral overtones that have long characterised food-related factual programming, particularly the fat-shaming weight loss programs that were prominent up to the mid-2010s.

Shows like *Crazy Delicious* and *Sugar Rush*, then, can be understood as part of what Jorie Lagerwey (2018) calls the "loving reality" genre of reality television. Loving reality, pioneered by broadcast programs such as *The Great British Bake Off*, represents a "collection of reality shows that foreground positive affects like love, friendship, and joy, emphasising them even over plot, character and competition or conflict" (Lagerwey 2018: 443). Loving reality is much gentler and kinder to contestants than programs that focus on harsh judging and a drive to 'win'. Contestants on loving reality shows are generally presented as enthusiastic amateurs participating simply for the love of cooking, rather than as using the show as a platform for any eventual professionalisation or celebritisation (Lagerwey 2018: 445). Although some loving reality contestants do become celebrities, such as *Bake Off*'s season 6 winner Nadiya Hussain, they are generally of what Lagerwey (2018: 444) refers to as the "amateur" sort—they are not terribly famous, and whatever fame they do accrue is essentially accidental, uncalculated, and unplanned.

Certainly, within the structures of shows like *Bake Off*, no suggestion exists that participants will create a self-brand or be professionalised into either baking or celebrity at the conclusion of filming. Instead, the payoff for participation is primarily presented as self-esteem, self-confidence, and friendship (Lagerwey 2018: 450). At the conclusion of each episode, considerable time is given over not to celebrating that week's star baker, but to consoling the eliminated contestant and reconstituting the group following the loss of a member (Lagerwey 2018: 451). As a result of its focus on positive forms of community, Lagerwey (2018: 446, 451) argues that the narrative conventions of loving reality result in a "de-emphasising [of] the self and the self-brand in favour of foregrounding positive affects", in ways that offer an "affective potential outside of the constant striving of neoliberal capitalism and its insistence on individual gain and individualised solutions to social problems".

Lagerwey reads such programs as a specifically British phenomenon, responding to specifically British social and political contexts (namely, the crises of the Brexit era). Through the harmonious social relations of their carefully constructed multicultural communities (including, for example, the hijab-wearing Nadiya), loving reality produces "inclusive images of nation" that offer respite from a political climate otherwise "suffused with hate and negative affect" (Lagerwey 2018: 443). While Lagerwey's reading of *The Great British Bake Off* in terms of nation is typical of analyses of the program (see Bradley 2016; Potter & Westall 2013 for similar arguments), her notion that shows such as *Bake Off* have opened the door for reality programming to operate in a positive affective register—as distinct from one of conflict and competitive individualism—is potentially useful for understanding reality programs outside any singular national context.

With their focus on positive judging, camaraderie between contestants, and general feel-good vibes, both *Crazy Delicious* and *Sugar Rush* extend many of the features of Lagerwey's "loving reality"—albeit with international streaming (rather than national broadcast) audiences in mind. The features of loving reality are perhaps most obvious in *Crazy Delicious*, with its lack of prizes and apparently amateur contestants (described in the opening credits as "inventive home cooks"). But they are also present in *Sugar Rush*, which (although played for prizes) largely downplays the importance of winning. In neither show do judges engage in the intense emotional badgering of contestants that can occur on other reality programs, even in otherwise 'collegial' shows such as *MasterChef*, where contestants are constantly asked to make uncomfortable personal disclosures, affirm their desire to win, and/or convince the judges to allow them to stay (Seale 2012: 34). Indeed, in neither show do we see contestants for long enough or know enough about them to become significantly invested in their successes or failures. Instead, the shows maintain interest through their Instagram-esque visual pleasures: the striking and creative dishes on *Crazy Delicious* and the impressive and beautifully presented bakes on *Sugar Rush*, the various components and techniques of which are generally described in more detail than the stories, successes, or failures of the contestants themselves.

If, as Lagerwey (2018) argues, celebrity is only an accidental product of loving reality shows, which otherwise contain few of the typical motors of celebrity production, then the need for contestants to cultivate a marketable self-brand is, if not eliminated, then at least significantly reduced. If so, this would seem to reflect a rather radical intervention in the narrative logics of reality television. Certainly, *Crazy Delicious*, *Sugar Rush*, and other similar shows (e.g. *Nailed It!*, *Best Leftovers Ever!*, *Cooked with Cannabis*) do not dramatise the processes of celebrity production—but this does not mean that the genre as a whole reflects a decline in the importance of self-branding. On the contrary, Netflix's reality cooking competitions seem to reflect a system in which both self-branding and the aspirational labour on which it is based have become so normalised that the development of a self-brand (and the celebrity that potentially comes along with it) is no longer a by-product of participation on reality television. Instead, a recognisable self-brand is increasingly a necessary precondition of participation in the first place.

Aspirational labour and the reframing of work

On *Crazy Delicious*, contestants may be billed as "inventive home cooks", but many of them also have significant followings on Instagram and run (varyingly profitable) micro-businesses based around content creation, brand endorsements, and/or home-based enterprises. For example, contestant Samira (who currently has 1 million Instagram followers, and had around 800,000 at the time of her *Crazy Delicious* appearance) works full-time on content creation, employs two staff, and earns "more money in one day from Instagram than in two months" in her previous role as a maths and physics tutor (Field 2018). A number of other contestants, including Chris (30.6K followers at the time of writing), Joseph (20.7K followers), and Bethie (28.4K followers), operate successfully as "micro-celebrities" (Khamis, Ang & Welling 2017), leveraging commercial opportunities from their food brands. Others still—such as Hardeep, Lara, and Elainea, with less than 10,000 followers each—operate mail-order food businesses, supper clubs, or workshops, and attempt in various ways to monetise their content creation. The contestants' distinctive 'food styles' that we see in the various episodes—such as Samira's rainbow-coloured vegetarian food, Chris' 'masculine' comfort food, and Elainea's Caribbean flavours—can also be found on their web and social media sites.

Framing the contestants as "inventive home cooks" presents their cookery as a form of leisure—when, in actuality, the contestants are (variously) fully professionalised, semi-professionalised, and wannabe-professionalised content producers, with all the real and aspirational labour this involves (Duffy 2017). As Brooke Erin Duffy's (2017: 96) study of fashion bloggers showed, the labour involved in digital content production is significant, and requires giving over a substantial amount of one's 'leisure' time to activities that look a great deal like traditional 'work'—albeit without the job security or stable remuneration. Indeed, the highly affective terms in which *Crazy Delicious* contestants describe their cooking not only replicate those of Duffy's (2017) fashion workers (who similarly describe their work as a source of love, passion, and creativity) but also those of an increasing number of workers in the contemporary informational economy more broadly.

As the growing scholarship in media and cultural studies on contemporary working conditions has shown, work has come to occupy an increasingly central position in the emotional and symbolic lives of subjects within the "new" informational economy (Gregg 2011; Hesmondhalgh & Baker 2010; McRobbie 2016). At a time when creative and digital industries, in particular, have largely abandoned traditional workplace protections in favour of precarious and exploitative forms of employment, workers have been required to adopt highly flexible, individualised modes of self-entrepreneurship and self-branding that frame work in highly affective terms—what Angela McRobbie (2016: 36) has termed "passionate work". In such a configuration, work becomes "akin to a romantic relationship", in which love for one's work essentially serves as a form of labour reform by stealth. "Passion" and "creativity" are the compensations for the loss of reasonable pay, leave entitlements, and secure employment under post-Fordist capitalism (McRobbie 2016: 3). As scholars have pointed out, the political power of these imperatives stems from the fact that, largely, they are not experienced as exploitation or alienation, despite the asymmetrical power relations involved (Kuehn & Corrigan 2013). Rather, they are experienced as a prospect of "do[ing] what [one] love[s]", where labour and leisure co-exist (Duffy 2017: 4).

McRobbie (2016: 91) understands this phenomenon in specifically gendered terms: she sees discourses of passionate work as producing normatively feminine forms of labour that govern female subjectivities in particular ways. But we can see in the passionate work that suffuses *Crazy Delicious* how disguising work as a leisure activity, done for passion or pleasure, can be used as a tool to normalise particular ideas about life and work for both women and men. Unlike *Crazy Delicious*, contestants on *Sugar Rush* are explicitly framed as the professional bakers they are, with the businesses they own or work for announced in the introduction for each team of contestants. However, there is nonetheless a similar blurring of the distinction between leisure and work. While presented as professionals, the contestants are framed not as the chef 'titans' that we tend to see in other media representations of cooking professionals, but as the rather ordinary owners or employees of modest small businesses or micro-enterprises, such as local bakeries or home-based baking businesses. Contestants will occasionally incorporate distinctive aspects of their business style or brand in one of their dishes, a notable example being Deborah's all-white peacock cake on *Season 3: Extra Sweet*. But, for the most part, the specifics of contestants' business identities form a relatively minor part of the show. Instead, contestants are encouraged to incorporate aspects of their personal identities into their bakes—their Hawaiian or Latin American heritage, for example, or their interest in music. While some teams are comprised of work colleagues, many are a combination of spouses, friends, and family members, and contestants typically state that opportunities for creativity and spending time with loved ones are their key motivators for participation. Consequently, although *Sugar Rush* presents its contestants as professional bakers, and its challenges ask them to demonstrate skills honed through their experiences of professional work, affective discourses of fun, leisure, and relationship-building are prioritised over more careerist aims within the show's narrative.

That commentators (and audiences) can construct these shows as "comforting" (Chayka 2020; Weissman 2019) is due in part to the fact that much of the labour underpinning contestants' 'ordinary' or 'amateur' identities remains invisible. If a key role of earlier forms of reality television was to dramatise the subjectivities necessary for success in neoliberal capitalism, shows like *Crazy Delicious* and *Sugar Rush* largely dispense with reality TV's disciplining and normalising pedagogies. Instead, socially desirable identities are no longer learned *through* shows like these, but are attributes that contestants come with already. In other words, streaming reality food competitions frequently represent not so much a sidelining of the importance of the self-brand, as Lagerwey (2018: 446) suggests of shows like *Bake Off*, but a different type of celebrity arc, in which the television show does not build a profile for the contestant, but rather contestants come with an already established personal and professional identity for the show to exploit.

If, as earlier scholarship has tended to read the genre, reality TV is an ideological arm of the post-welfare state (Ouellette & Hay 2008a, 2008b; Redden 2018), then *Crazy Delicious* and *Sugar Rush* represent an end-point in which neoliberal governmentality has become so normalised that its explicit narrativisation is no longer necessary. Rather than teaching contestants (and, by extension, audiences) to be 'good' cooks or 'good' bakers or 'good' citizens, such shows leverage the significant work of identity production undertaken prior to contestants' appearances on these shows. That contestants undertake this labour seemingly for pleasure—the pleasure of cooking, or simply of being "chosen" or "valid[ated]", in the words of one *Sugar Rush* contestant—is part of what gives audiences frictionless viewing. But contestants presumably also undertake this labour for the promotional opportunities that appearances on such shows provide to present and translate their brand across different media platforms. The fact that participating on the show can help promote contestants' existing off-screen businesses allows Netflix to benefit not just from contestants' free labour *within* the shows (as per the traditional model of reality TV) but also from contestants' additional labour in driving existing audiences and followers *to* the show. In contrast to the secrecy that surrounds contestant selection on broadcast reality shows like *MasterChef* and *My Kitchen Rules*, contestants on *Crazy Delicious* and *Sugar Rush* almost always announced their involvement in the show well in advance of their episode—and to their (often significant numbers of) followers on social media. Many contestants (especially on *Sugar Rush*) also sought additional promotional opportunities with local media, finding many outlets eager to celebrate local businesses gaining a profile on the international stage.

The result is not so much about educating people in cookery, or even in the art of lifestyle, as about extracting as much value as possible from contestants and (ultimately) audiences. By selecting contestants with already established businesses, identities, and audiences—albeit ones ordinary and aspirational enough as not to warrant significant appearance fees or overshadow those of the judges or hosts—Netflix food shows leverage the promotional labour undertaken by contestants while simultaneously framing this work as a pleasurable form of leisure. This is not the case for all Netflix Original programming (an obvious exception is *Nailed It!*, with its hilariously unskilled amateur bakers)—but the formula of free labour, often masked by the relentless cheerfulness of contestants, hosts, and judges, is a feature of shows ranging from *Best Leftovers Ever!* to *Cooked with Cannabis*, each of which features similarly 'low-level' professional chefs and cooks as *Crazy Delicious* and *Sugar Rush*.

The work of watching

The repetition of notions of work-as-leisure is significant not just for the ways in which it dramatises the immaterial labour that is now central to work in contemporary capitalism (Hardt & Negri 2004), but also for the ways in which these narratives of uncompensated contestant labour parallel (and, in many ways, normalise and obscure) the *audience* labour that is now essential to the business model of digital platforms like Netflix. In this respect, it becomes necessary to understand how narratives within streaming television reflect and are shaped by the contexts and infrastructures that give rise to them: to understand, as Bellanova and González Fuster (2018: 227) describe it, both "what is brought and performed on-stage and what is performed and done to create the stage itself".

A significant body of scholarship now outlines the ways in which the extraction of value from audience labour is fundamental to digital capitalism (Andrejevic 2007; Kuehn & Corrigan 2013; Ross 2013; Terranova 2000). For platforms like Netflix, audience practices are revenue-producing in the sense that every action undertaken on the platform operates as a source of "transactional data that is available for companies to harvest and data mine", often without audiences' full understanding of what is occurring (Beer & Burrows 2010: 9; see also Bellanova & González Fuster 2018: 231; Floegel 2021: 222; Stehling et al. 2018: 82). As Diana Floegel (2021) argues, the immateriality of audience activity means that it is often not recognised *as labour*—but audiences' work is nonetheless essential to the productivity of digital media industries, by helping to refine algorithms, advance systems design, and inform the production and promotion of program content (Floegel 2021: 216). Algorithmically driven audience activity can have a significant influence in production decisions, such as determining key subject matter, directors, or actors (as in *House of Cards* and

Orange is the New Black). It can also shape strategies for promotion: for example, the decision to promote the white, male Jacques Torres in thumbnail images of *Nailed It!* over his black, female co-host Nicole Beyer reflected algorithmic insights about the market value of 'whiteness' for mainstream audiences, in ways that reveal the "inequities that are instantiated in sociotechnical systems" (Floegel 2021: 219, 221, 222). In these respects, Netflix audiences cannot be viewed simply as *consumers* of content; they are also *co-producers* both of content and the data that underpin it (Bellanova & González Fuster 2018: 242).

That this production work is done without the capacity for compensation or reward (beyond viewers' own entertainment or the potential to 'personalise' their experience) is central to Netflix's exploitation of audience labour (Bellanova & González Fuster 2018: 229; Floegel 2021: 216). That Netflix accumulates value by presenting this audience labour as *not work* parallels the free-labouring, value-generating capacities of its on-screen contestants. In both cases, the pleasurable reframing of work-as-leisure enrols participants, both on- and off-screen, in digitally mediated dynamics of affective capture in which the boundaries between life, work, and play are increasingly blurred (Pilipets 2019: 1). While (semi-)professionalised reality contestants incur financial costs for the privilege of participation, fee-paying subscribers labour for free to build and refine platform infrastructure. Netflix's leveraging of both contestant and audience labour highlights the ways in which bodies, brands, and technologies are now brought into connection in ways that reproduce inequalities that the program content would (on the surface) seem to resist.

While shows like *Crazy Delicious* and *Sugar Rush* may, at a textual level, invoke harmonious depictions of equality and diversity, at the production level they are based on extracting value from audiences, as well as content and identities from platforms (notably Instagram) that are themselves highly normative. Success on Instagram often depends on conformity to conventionally attractive, white (and sometimes Asian) personas that dovetail with existing marketing discourses (Duffy 2017: 184; Marwick 2015). Moreover, success in content creation is rarely open to those without the resources to work for free, either in a temporary or an ongoing capacity (Duffy 2017: 96). These more sobering realities would seem to disrupt much of the progressive potential that shows like *Crazy Delicious* and *Sugar Rush* appear to offer. The texts may depict diversely gendered, aged, classed, and raced participants engaging in joyous 'amateur' creativity—but at production and infrastructural levels, the shows capitalise on pre-existing businesses, brands, and content, as well as enrolling taste communities in algorithmic labour that can be increasingly understood as exploitative. If media systems and the data on which they depend operate as forms of governance that simultaneously enact subjectivity and produce populations (Beer & Burrows 2013: 50), they do this by both limiting and directing action in ways that oscillate between "exploitation and recognition, pleasure and profits" (Stehling et al. 2018: 92–93). For Miriam Stehling and colleagues (2018: 85), it is thus essential to think about audiences' digital labour alongside the co-optation of their work and data enabled by digital technologies—to which I would add the necessity of thinking about the labour of reality contestants, whose revenue-generating activities before and after appearing on the show are equally imbricated in the production economy of contemporary reality television.

Over a decade ago, Andrew Ross (2009: 136) described reality TV as an example of the ongoing restructuring of the creative industries, designed to profit from the skills and production of un- and underpaid workers. "The overriding factor in shaping reality television's industrial profile," he wrote, "is the drive on the part of producers and owners to slice costs by eroding or circumventing work standards" for both contestants and production staff (Ross 2014: 30). While "slic[ing] costs" has long been central to the political economy of reality television, newer forms of streaming reality TV are outsourcing even more of the costs of production and promotion to contestants and audiences. If earlier forms of reality television essentially served as a template for labour on the self, with the work involved in producing oneself as a marketable self-brand central to program narratives, in streaming reality, contestants are no longer just a source of cheap labour who offer an 'amateur' point of identification for audiences. Instead, streaming reality depends on contestants to leverage their previous work of identity production and professional skill development, bring existing audiences and followers with them, and engage in more expansive forms of promotional labour—while still being framed as essentially 'amateur'. Equally, the political economy of contemporary reality TV increasingly depends on the enthusiasm of audience "taste communities" (Lotz 2021: 893) prepared to undertake unpaid production and promotional work, for both the contestants and the platform infrastructures that depend on their uncompensated labour.

That the labour of both audiences and contestants is understood not as work, but in affective terms of creativity, pleasure, and "comfort", highlights the extent to which the textual, production, and infrastructural conventions of streaming reality reflect an endpoint in neoliberal capitalism, whereby (self-)exploitation has now become so normalised that narrativising or justifying its processes (long understood to be one of the key ideological and affective functions of earlier forms of reality TV) is no longer required. Such programs, then, offer revealing examples of the extent to which un- and underpaid labour has become so embedded in contemporary digital capitalism that neither audiences nor contestants any longer need to be convinced of its necessity or inevitability. Yet the prospect that this un- and underpaid work can be experienced not just as necessary or inevitable but as a source of *comfort*—"warm, sun-kissed, and generally uplifting" (Weissman 2019)—reflects a significant reframing of affective experiences of labour in a digital era.

The politics of streaming reality

On competition reality programs like *Crazy Delicious* and *Sugar Rush*, audiences and contestants are mobilised not through the coercive forms of discipline and control that were the stock-in-trade of network-era reality television, but rather through ideological messaging that goes 'under the radar' of experiences of pleasure and comfort. Such shows highlight the relationships between textual conventions that collapse distinctions between labour and leisure, production practices that leverage existing audiences and professional identities, and algorithmic logics powered by uncompensated audience labour. In this confluence of textual representations, production practices, and platform infrastructures, digital television texts produce particular types of meaning and affect, operate via hidden vectors of power and control, and work to support specific platform logics. That Netflix consistently prioritises certain types of reality programming over others simultaneously constructs the Netflix brand as synonymous with easy-going, feel-good entertainment—resisting the cynicism and "cheap pathos" of its broadcast and cable competitors (Weismann 2019)—and shows how its production and curatorial decisions have been carefully designed to support its own platform logics and economies.

As this chapter has argued, these production and curatorial decisions, each with their particular textual, industrial, and infrastructural e/affects, disrupt many of our established scholarly understandings of how reality TV works for—and on—both contestants and audiences. However, while the politics of Netflix cooking competitions may be difficult to capture within the conventional disciplinary and pedagogical frameworks through which we have typically understood reality television, this does not mean that such programs perform no ideological work or disciplining of viewers or contestants. In fact, their ideological work may be all the more powerful for their 'feel-good' presentation, highlighting the ways in which the neoliberal investment in the self is now increasingly promoted without explicit narration or dramatisation.

This locates the power and politics of contemporary reality TV in quite a different place from that which we may have identified previously. Earlier programs like *MasterChef*, with its dentists and lawyers vying to give up their secure, highly-paid jobs for a chance at a more 'fulfilling' career in food, undoubtedly glamorised professional cooking in ways that obscured the far less appealing realities of hospitality industry work (Kirkwood & Phillipov 2015). In contrast, the flattening of intensity, modest aspirations, and positive reframing of unpaid labour as a form of 'comfort', on shows like *Crazy Delicious* and *Sugar Rush*, mean that contemporary food TV no longer presents its contestants as sacrificing pay and conditions for a new career that they 'love', but rather as conceiving their work to be so inherently rewarding that it no longer requires any compensation at all. Thus such programs, paradoxically, seem to normalise even more insidious ideologies of contemporary work than those where the exploitation of contestants was more explicit.

Moreover, the algorithmic logics of streaming television may extend the ideological reach of these programs in unexpected ways. Netflix's recommendation system may well direct viewers of *Crazy Delicious* and *Sugar Rush* to other cooking competitions or similarly formatted food shows (e.g. *Best Leftovers Ever!, Nailed It!, Cooked with Cannabis*). But it is just as likely to suggest other Netflix Original and licensed content (e.g. *The Big Flower Fight, Blown Away, Next in Fashion, Interior Design Masters, Glow Up*) that adopts the conventions of "loving reality" but transfers its affects to other activities and subjects. From flower arranging and glass blowing to fashion design and make-up art, we are seeing an algorithmic proliferation of shows equally reliant on a combination of professionalised, semi-professionalised, and not-yet-professionalised labour, and which have equally been read as "comforting" and "soothing" viewing (e.g. Adegoke 2020; Bruney 2020; Bundel 2020).

This highlights not just how powerfully affective experiences of comfort can be created through production practices and infrastructures essentially designed for exploitation, but also how food TV's affects can be transferred to a whole range of other activities. And it is perhaps no accident that such activities are concentrated in hospitality and creative industries, which have been most vulnerable to the erosion of industrial relations and where many struggle to make a secure living. As a result, shows like *Crazy Delicious* and *Sugar Rush* highlight the significant expansion and normalisation of streaming reality TV's reliance on un- and underpaid contestant and audience labour, as well as the ways in which soothing and comforting affects can be employed to mask these more unsavoury realities. The examples in this chapter have revealed how streaming reality's dampening down of intensity is crucial to achieving and normalising its (political) affects. The next chapter will explore food television's affective forces more fully by considering the ways in which other types of digital food TV—in this case, online food videos—gain their power and significance not through the flattening of affect, but through its intensification.

Note

1 Netflix's ten largest markets are: the US, Brazil, UK, Mexico, France, Canada, Germany, Australia, Argentina, and Spain (Statista 2019). *Crazy Delicious* is not licensed for Netflix in the UK due to its broadcast deal with Channel 4.

References

Adegoke, Yomi 2020, 'Bake Off and beyond: The unstoppable rise of craft reality TV', *The Guardian Australia*, 18 December, https://www.theguardian.com/tv-and-radio/2020/dec/17/bake-off-and-beyond-the-unstoppable-rise-of-crafty-reality-tv. Accessed 13 July 2021.

Andrejevic, Mark 2007, *iSpy: Surveillance and Power in the Interactive Era*. University Press of Kansas: Lawrence.

Ashley, Bob, Hollows, Joanne, Jones, Steve & Taylor, Ben 2004, *Food and Cultural Studies*. Routledge: London.

Beer, David & Burrows, Roger 2010, 'Consumption, presumption and participatory web cultures: An introduction', *Journal of Consumer Culture*, vol. 10, no. 1, pp. 3–12. https://doi.org/10.1177/1469540509354009

Beer, David & Burrows, Roger 2013, 'Popular culture, digital archives and the new social life of data', *Theory, Culture & Society*, vol. 30, no. 4, pp. 47–71. https://doi.org/10.1177/0263276413476542

Bell, David & Hollows, Joanne (eds) 2005, *Ordinary Lifestyles: Popular Media, Consumption and Taste*. Open University Press: Maidenhead.

Bellanova, Rocco & González Fuster, Gloria 2018, 'No (big) data, no fiction? Thinking surveillance with/against Netflix'. In Ann Rudinow Sætnan, Ingrid Schneider & Nicola Green (eds), *The Politics and Policies of Big Data: Big Data Big Brother?* Routledge: London, pp. 227–246.

Bennett, James & Holmes, Su 2010, 'The "place" of television in celebrity studies', *Celebrity Studies*, vol. 1, no. 1, pp. 65–80. https://doi.org/10.1080/19392390903519073

Birch, Kean 2015, 'Neoliberalism: The whys and wherefores... and future directions', *Sociology Compass*, vol. 9, no. 7, pp. 571–584. https://doi.org/10.1111/soc4.12277

Boltanski, Luc & Chiapello, Eve 2005, *The New Spirit of Capitalism*. Verso: London.

Bonner, Frances 2003, *Ordinary Television: Analyzing Popular TV*. Sage: London.

Bonner, Frances 2005, 'Looking inside: Showing medical operations on ordinary television'. In Geoff King (ed.), *The Spectacle of the Real: From Hollywood to Reality TV and Beyond*. University of Chicago Press: Chicago, IL, pp. 105–116.

Bradley, Peri 2016, 'More cake please—we're British! Locating British identity in contemporary TV food texts, *The Great British Bake Off* and *Come Dine With Me*'. In Peri Bradley (ed.), *Food, Media and Contemporary Culture: The Edible Image*. Palgrave Macmillan: Houndmills, pp. 9–26.

Brearley, Max 2018, 'Netflix has revolutionised food TV—and the tired Australian networks need to tune in', *The Guardian Australia*, 13 December, https://www.theguardian.com/media/2018/dec/13/netflix-has-revolutionised-food-tv-and-the-tired-australian-networks-need-to-tune-in. Accessed 14 January 2022.

Bruney, Gabrielle 2020, '*The Big Flower Fight* is a glorious escape for those of us trapped inside', *Esquire*, 18 May, https://www.esquire.com/entertainment/tv/a32501767/the-big-flower-fight-review-cast-netflix/. Accessed 13 July 2021.

Bundel, Ani 2020, 'These 20 reality competition shows are perfect for a soothing self-care day', *Elite Daily*, 5 November, https://www.elitedaily.com/p/20-soothing-competition-shows-to-stream-when-you-want-to-forget-your-problems-41523532. Accessed 13 July 2021.

Chayka, Kyle 2020, '"Emily in Paris" and the rise of ambient TV', *The New Yorker*, 16 November, https://www.newyorker.com/culture/cultural-comment/emily-in-paris-and-the-rise-of-ambient-tv. Accessed 14 January 2022.

Duffy, Brooke Erin 2017, *(Not) Getting Paid to Do What You Love: Gender, Social Media, and Aspirational Work*. Yale University Press: New Haven, CT & London.

Field, Hayden 2018, 'This college professor makes more money in one day from Instagram than in two months teaching. Here are her secrets to success', *Entrepreneur*, 2 May, https://www.entrepreneur.com/article/312853. Accessed 25 February 2021.

Floegel, Diana 2021, 'Labor, classification and productions of culture on Netflix', *Journal of Documentation*, vol. 77, no. 1, pp. 209–228. https://doi.org/10.1108/JD-06-2020-0108

Gregg, Melissa 2011, *Work's Intimacy*. Cambridge: Polity.

Hardt, Michael & Negri, Antonio 2004, *Multitude: War and Democracy in the Age of Empire*. Penguin Books: New York.

Hearn, Alison 2008a, 'Insecure: Narratives and economies of the branded self in transformation television', *Continuum: Journal of Media & Cultural Studies*, vol. 22, no. 4, pp. 495–504. https://doi.org/10.1080/10304310802189972

Hearn, Alison 2008b, '"Meat, mask, burden": Probing the contours of the branded "self"', *Journal of Consumer Culture*, vol. 8, no. 2, pp. 197–217. https://doi.org/10.1177/1469540508090086

Hearn, Alison 2014, 'Producing "Reality": Branded content, branded selves, precarious futures'. In Laurie Ouellette (ed.), *A Companion to Reality Television*. Wiley Blackwell: Malden, pp. 437–455.

Hesmondhalgh, David & Baker, Sarah 2010, '"A very complicated version of freedom": Conditions and experiences of creative labour in three cultural industries', *Poetics*, vol. 38, no. 1, pp. 4–20. https://doi.org/10.1016/j.poetic.2009.10.001

Johanssen, Jacob 2017, 'Immaterial labour and reality TV: The affective surplus of excess'. In Marco Briziarella & Emiliana Armano (eds), *The Spectacle 2.0: Reading Debord in the Context of Digital Capitalism*. University of Westminster Press: London, pp. 197–208.

Kavka, Misha 2014, 'A matter of feeling: Mediated affect in reality television'. In Laurie Ouellette (ed.), *A Companion to Reality Television*. Wiley Blackwell: Malden, pp. 459–477.

Khamis, Susie, Ang, Lawrence & Welling, Raymond 2017, 'Self-branding, "micro-celebrity" and the rise of social media influencers', *Celebrity Studies*, vol. 8, no. 2, pp. 191–208. https://doi.org/10.1080/19392397.2016.1218292

Kirkwood, Katherine & Phillipov, Michelle 2015, 'What MasterChef teaches us about food and the food industry', *The Conversation*, 21 May, https://theconversation.com/what-masterchef-teaches-us-about-food-and-the-food-industry-41893. Accessed 14 January 2022.

Kuehn, Kathleen & Corrigan, Thomas F. 2013, 'Hope labor: The role of employment prospects in online social production', *The Political Economy of Communication*, vol. 1, no. 1, pp. 9–25. https://polecom.org/index.php/polecom/article/view/9

Lagerwey, Jorie 2018, '*The Great British Bake Off*, joy, and the affective potential of Nadiya Hussain's amateur celebrity', *Celebrity Studies*, vol. 9, no. 4, pp. 442–454. https://doi.org/10.1080/19392397.2018.1508964

Lewis, Tania 2008, *Smart Living: Lifestyle Media and Popular Expertise*. Peter Lang: New York.

Lewis, Tania 2011, '"You've put yourself on a plate": The labours of selfhood on *MasterChef Australia*'. In Beverley Skeggs & Helen Wood (eds), *Reality Television and Class*. Palgrave Macmillan: London, pp. 104–116.

Lotz, Amanda 2021, 'Unpopularity and cultural power in the age of Netflix: New questions for cultural studies' approaches to television texts', *European Journal of Cultural Studies*, vol. 24, no. 4, pp. 887–900. https://doi.org/10.1177/1367549421994578

Marwick, Alice E. 2015, 'Instafame: Luxury selfies in the attention economy', *Public Culture*, vol. 27, no. 1, pp. 137–160. https://doi.org/10.1215/08992363-2798379

McRobbie, Angela 2016, *Be Creative: Making a Living in the New Culture Industries*. Polity: London.

Miller, Toby 2007, *Cultural Citizenship: Cosmopolitanism, Consumerism and Television in a Neoliberal Age*. Temple University Press: Philadelphia, PA.

Moseley, Rachel 2001, '"Real lads do cook....but some things are still hard to talk about": The gendering of 8–9', *European Journal of Cultural Studies*, vol. 4, no. 1, pp. 32–39. https://doi.org/10.1177/136754940100400102

Neff, Gina 2012, *Venture Labor: Work and the Burden of Risk in Innovative Industries*. The MIT Press: Cambridge.

Oren, Tasha 2013, 'On the line: Format, cooking and competition as television values', *Critical Studies in Television*, vol. 8, no. 2, pp. 20–35. https://doi.org/10.7227/CST.8.2.3

Ouellette, Laurie & Hay, James 2008a, *Better Living through Reality TV: Television and Post-Welfare Citizenship*. Blackwell: Malden, MA.

Ouellette, Laurie & Hay, James 2008b, 'Makeover television, governmentality and the good citizen', *Continuum: Journal of Media & Cultural Studies*, vol. 22, no. 4, pp. 471–484. https://doi.org/10.1080/10304310801982930

Palmer, Gareth 2004, '"The new you": Class and transformation in lifestyle television'. In Su Holmes & Deborah Jermyn (eds), *Understanding Reality Television*. Routledge: London, pp. 173–190.

Pilipets, Elena 2019, 'From Netflix and streaming to Netflix and chill: The (dis)connected body of the serial binge-viewer', *Social Media + Society*, vol. 5, no. 4, pp. 1–13. https://doi.org/10.1177/2056305119883426

Potter, Lucy & Westall, Claire 2013, 'Neoliberal Britain's austerity foodscape: Home economics, veg patch capitalism and culinary temporality', *New Formations*, vol. 80–81, pp. 155–178. https://www.muse.jhu.edu/article/529458.

Redden, Guy 2018, 'Is reality TV neoliberal?', *Television & New Media*, vol. 19, no. 5, pp. 399–414. https://doi.org/10.1177/1527476417728377

Ross, Andrew 2009, 'The political economy of amateurism', *Television & New Media*, vol. 10, no. 1, pp. 136–137. https://doi.org/10.1177/1527476408325723

Ross, Andrew 2013, 'In search of the lost paycheck'. In Trebor Scholz (ed.), *Digital Labor: The Internet as Playground and Factory*. Routledge: New York, pp. 13–32.

Ross, Andrew 2014, 'Reality television and the political economy of amateurism'. In Laurie Ouellette (ed.), *A Companion to Reality Television*. Wiley Blackwell: Malden, pp. 29–39.

Seale, Kirsten 2012, '*MasterChef*'s amateur makeovers', *Media International Australia*, no. 143, pp. 28–35. https://doi.org/10.1177/1329878X1214300105

Skeggs, Beverley & Wood, Helen (eds) 2011, *Reality Television and Class*. Palgrave Macmillan: London.

Statista 2019, 'Leading Netflix markets worldwide in 2019', https://www.statista.com/statistics/499844/netflix-markets-penetration/. Accessed 25 February 2021.

Stehling, Miriam, Vesnić-Alujević, Lucia, Jorge, Ana & Marôpo, Lidia 2018, 'The co-option of audience data and user-generated content: Empowerment and exploitation amidst algorithms, produsage and crowdsourcing'. In Ranjana Das & Brita Ytre-Arne (eds), *The Future of Audiences: A Foresight*

Analysis of Interfaces and Engagement. Palgrave Macmillan: Cham, pp. 79–99.

Terranova, Tiziana 2000, 'Free labor: Producing culture for the digital economy', *Social Text*, vol. 63, no. 18, pp. 33–58. https://doi.org/10.1215/01642472-18-2_63-33

Weissman, Cale Guthrie 2019, 'Meet the executives who have made Netflix food TV', *Business Insider*, 25 February, https://www.fastcompany.com/90310413/how-netflix-became-the-new-food-network. Accessed 14 January 2022.

Wood, Helen & Skeggs, Beverley 2011, 'Introduction: Real class'. In Beverley Skeggs & Helen Wood (eds), *Reality Television and Class*. Palgrave Macmillan: London, pp. 1–29.

3 Affect switches
Affective capture and market logics in online food videos

Scrolling through my Facebook feed one morning while eating breakfast, I watch disembodied hands preparing a four-tiered layer cake. Pale turquoise frosting is carefully applied to each layer, the turntable spinning mesmerically until the cake is perfectly symmetrical and smooth. Drip effects in a darker shade of turquoise slide gently down the sides of the cake before it is topped with an artfully placed waffle cone filled with coloured popcorn, flowers, and giant gold cachous. The baker's hands then prepare another cake, this one with ombre rainbow frosting, topped with halved wafer cones filled with white buttercream mimicking the texture of soft serve. White chocolate ganache spills from the cones and drips down the sides of the cake, giving the illusion of melting ice cream.

The video, 'These cakes are called PERFECTION' (113K views at the time of writing), is a sponsored post by MetDaan Cakes, one of a growing number of content aggregators whose posts have become an increasingly common feature of Facebook newsfeeds (Patel 2016). With Facebook now the dominant player in the video marketing space (Cunningham, Craig & Silver 2016: 381), there has been a proliferation of operators like MetDaan creating short, instructional how-to videos and helpful hacks compiled from the work of (mostly YouTube-based) online content creators. Material generated by content aggregators sits alongside that of a growing number of digital-first publishers and MCNs (multi-channel networks), such as Tasty and Tastemade, that produce bespoke content ideal for silent, distracted scrolling and optimised to integrate advertising seamlessly into Facebook's native flow (Brodmerkel & Carah 2016: 102).

The proliferation of short-form food videos is an example of the ways in which Facebook's socially connective affordances now occur in highly commercialised settings. But despite their obviously commercial logics, there is something about these videos that is pleasurably

DOI: 10.4324/9781003261940-4

and inexplicably compelling—and I am not the only one to find them so. "Mesmerizing", "captivat[ing]", "seductive", "compulsively watchable": these are just some of the terms that have been used to describe the soothing, almost hypnotising, experience of watching online food videos (Evans 2016; Greenberg 2016). Writing for *The Cut*, Dayna Evans (2016) describes watching Tasty videos—by far the largest of the online food publishing brands with more than 100M Facebook followers—as moments of Zen-like meditation. She does not cook any of the recipes she watches, but the videos nonetheless provide a calming salve for frayed nerves. As she writes:

> They tap into the pleasure center of my brain with their mesmerizing simplicity, lack of fussiness, and quick pace... In a sea of free-flowing content hitting my already-scattered brain (often without my asking), Tasty videos act as calming one-minute meditations.
>
> (Evans 2016)

In *Wired*, Julia Greenberg (2016) describes the challenges of trying to write while being distracted by a "waking Facebook dream of cheesy French pull-apart bread and whiskey iced tea, ice cream donut holes and pulled pork porchetta sandwiches". "I watched clip after clip", she writes. "I wasn't particularly hungry. I wasn't particularly bored. And I definitely won't be making any of them myself. But ... I was captivated" (Greenberg 2016).

Such experiences of meditation and captivation are interesting given that many of these videos, with their clear ingredients lists, measurements, and methods, seem far more useful as basic cookery instruction than as entertainment—especially when compared with the more lavish Netflix offerings analysed in Chapter 2. The simple Greek yoghurt dips and stuffed zucchinis that so enthralled Evans, the easy-bake artichokes and honey BBQ chicken wings that so captivated Greenberg—all could easily serve as quick and fuss-free recipe ideas for everyday family meals: in other words, as a source of practical inspiration rather than sustained engagement. Indeed, approaching the videos as primarily instructional would seem to reflect the ways in which both scholars and marketers typically understand users' engagement with short-form food content. Research by Google revealed that 59% of millennials use their smartphones or tablets for every stage of the cooking process, consulting their mobile devices for recipe ideas, videos, cooking instructions, and real-time guidance while preparing meals (Cooper 2015). Such conclusions have been confirmed

Affect switches: Affective capture and market logics 67

by ethnographic research, which highlights the "growing colonization of kitchens by smartphones, laptops, and tablets", with people using their devices to access recipes and how-to videos while cooking (Lewis 2020: 67). Tania Lewis' study of household digital media use found short-form food content to be low on entertainment value, largely concerned with instruction, and "highly attuned to the pragmatic needs and everyday habits and practices of households" (Lewis 2020: 63). Katherine Kirkwood (2018: 285, 286) came to similar conclusions in her investigation of food media use in Brisbane households: participants tended to use digital food media (particularly YouTube and Facebook videos) less for entertainment or leisure than for more pragmatic reasons, such as looking up a recipe or mastering a cookery skill or technique.

The place of digital food content in everyday cultures of use has prompted calls from scholars to investigate the significance of food videos not through text-based analyses of representations or narratives, but through approaches that recognise media as practice (Couldry 2004; Morley 2009). As Tania Lewis (2020: 68) argues, adequate understanding of online food videos requires:

> [a] shift from media studies' usual focus on meaning making, audiences and institutions to thinking about the ways in which people use technologies (such as laptops and smartphones) and content (such as 'how to' videos on YouTube) in their daily lives and how this intersects with a range of other practices (i.e., using online food advice to cook a quick meal while looking after the kids after a long day at work).

In other words, understanding online food videos necessitates moving beyond textual 'readings' to a more embedded, ethnographic approach to the incorporation of digital media into everyday lives. But while ethnographic studies are certainly much needed, this chapter seeks to explore the ways in which textual analysis of online food texts might also contribute to understandings of their significance and use. With some notable exceptions (e.g. Lewis 2020; Lupton 2020), close textual analysis of online food videos is relatively rare in food media studies. But if, as commentators have suggested, one of the uses of online food videos is to elicit relaxation and meditation, it is likely that these affective states are produced, at least in part, by the videos' textual conventions. Adequate understanding of these conventions and their impacts does indeed require a shift away from "media studies' usual focus" (Lewis 2020: 68)—and this includes understanding food media texts as carriers not just of meanings, representations, and narratives, but also of affects.

In this chapter, I argue that while online food videos may appear to be instructional, and while (in many cases) they adopt 'classic' conventions of earlier food television forms, their uses and pleasures also derive from sonic and visual triggers that exceed the representational logics of these texts. These triggers generate "vitalities and visceralities" (Lupton 2019: 151), reframing online food videos as not simply texts to be viewed or watched, but sources of affective force and intensity that locate the viewer *in* the video through embodied experiences of the materialities of food and cooking. This suggests a different kind of politics for these newer televisual texts, compared with what our earlier analytical approaches have typically allowed. In order to explore this, the chapter focuses on online baking videos drawn from a range of genres and sources, including content aggregators, MCNs (multi-channel networks), and producers of ASMR (Autonomous Sensory Meridian Response). The focus on baking is, in part, due to its long-standing cultural connotations of care, relaxation, and comfort, which potentially lend baking videos a greater capacity for the captivating and mesmeric affects that commentators describe. But I also focus on baking because its significant popularity as an online cooking genre, and corresponding capacity for sponsored content and branded tie-ins (Think with Google 2016), make it a useful site for exploring the tensions between user-generated and commercial agendas that now characterise online video (Cunningham & Craig 2019).

The chapter begins by outlining the narrative and generic connections between online food videos and earlier forms of instructional food television, but shows how online videos are also generative of affects that expand the conceptual and analytical boundaries of food TV—and, indeed, what constitutes 'cooking' and 'eating'. It then uses Sven Brodmerkel and Nicholas Carah's (2016) concept of "brand machines" to show how online food videos' affective forces operate by creating touch points between bodies and calculative media systems, which can be put into the service of both progressive and reactionary ends. The chapter argues that attention to the specific textuality of food videos allows us to better understand the operation of digital food texts in assembling food, bodies, and technologies. This attention also helps us to understand the role of such texts in producing new biopolitics of food and modalities of food media, as well as affective forces that move (and potentially capture) bodies in ways that cannot always be identified in advance.

Instructional TV

Although I would argue that online food videos operate as digitally specific carriers of affect, there are nonetheless notable continuities between online food videos and earlier media forms, particularly broadcast food television. In her recent book *Digital Food*, Tania Lewis (2020: 47, 54) traces contemporary online food videos as an extension of the "ordinary expertise" of earlier forms of lifestyle media. She highlights the ways in which the participatory ethos and affordances of video-sharing platforms like YouTube have enabled a diverse range of digital culinary intermediaries (including 'ordinary' home cooks and people with niche, specialist culinary skills) to attract audiences and connect globally over the topic of food. Reading instructional food videos as digital versions of "Cookery-Educative" food programs, as Niki Strange (1998: 301) terms them, Lewis argues that such videos often explicitly draw from the stand-and-stir conventions of early forms of food television—albeit supplanting the well-known celebrity host with an 'ordinary' home cook, and replacing the pseudo-domestic settings of the TV studio with the real (and often far less stylish) kitchens of householders (Lewis 2020: 61, 62).

The parallels between online food videos and traditional forms of food TV are even more marked in YouTube's increasingly professionalised food channels. Early scholarship typically framed YouTube as a haven for non-commercial, amateur content (e.g. Strangelove 2010). Yet the platform, with its "micro-celebrities" and native-to-online sponsored content, has long blurred distinctions between commercial and user-generated media (Burgess & Green 2018; Cunningham & Craig 2019; Marwick 2016; van Dijck 2013). YouTube's unique combination of content—amateur, "professionalising amateur", professional, and branded (Cunningham & Craig 2019: 5)—has been shaped in part by Google's drive to make YouTube "more like TV", as a strategy for enhancing its appeal to advertisers and media partners (Lobato 2016: 348; see also Burgess & Green 2018: 20). Indeed, a growing number of popular YouTube food channels could easily be read as digital-first versions of content that would otherwise be at home on network television. For example, YouTube's most successful baking channel, Rosanna Pansino's Nerdy Nummies (12.8M subscribers), engages the audience through personalised modes of address that anchor it in YouTube's values of authenticity and community (Burgess & Green 2018). But Nerdy Nummies also mimics a range of 'classic' food television conventions, such as the direct address to camera, a regular rotation of 'special guests', professional opening title sequences, and rapid, crisp editing. With Pansino's chirpy, animated personality and appealing good looks, her videos could easily be seen not just as examples of the "Cookery-Educative" mode of food TV, but also of "Personality" (Strange 1998: 304), in which the host's identity provides a key dimension of the show's appeal.

As Nerdy Nummies has grown in popularity, its offerings have come to look increasingly like those of network TV. Over time, Pansino's kitchen has evolved from the more homely setting it was when the channel first launched in 2011, to one with high-end appliances, marble surfaces, and professional lighting. In fact, much of Nerdy Nummies' current content would now seem at home on any Food Network offering, and Pansino's YouTube success has seen her launch a more conventional media career, with book deals, TV hosting, and mainstream media appearances. This has seen her operate more like the "entertainment packages" (Ashley et al. 2004: 175) of broadcast-era celebrity chefs than as a YouTube-specific celebrity—a role, some have suggested, that is "rigorously differentiated from established professional media" (Cunningham & Craig 2019: 149).

Despite YouTube's vast array of diverse, amateur content (Burgess & Green 2018; Strangelove 2010), the most successful online channels often conform to mainstream media and marketing norms. This includes a predominance of lifestyle content (such as beauty, food, fashion, and fitness) that can easily be matched with brands, and the disproportionate visibility of photogenic, middle-class content creators with personas compatible with advertisers' demands and needs (Bishop 2018: 71; see also Duffy 2017: 103). In the world of online cooking and baking videos, many of the most successful creators offer an ideal combination of authenticity and enthusiasm, as well as the conventionally marketable traits of physical attractiveness and aspirational appeal. For example, watching a video of Rosanna Pansino preparing a birthday party for her French Bulldog, Coconut, in her rather opulent new home ('Throwing My Dog an EPIC Birthday Party!', 1.2M views), it becomes possible to understand such forms of food celebrity as digital-first versions of the charismatic—and conventionally marketable—hosts of broadcast food television, where the likes of Jamie Oliver or Nigella Lawson instruct viewers not just in the art of cooking, but also in the art of desirable and aspirational lifestyle.

Understanding online food videos as extensions of earlier forms of food TV reveals the ways in which 'classic' TV conventions are maintained and adapted within online-only contexts, and highlights the ongoing continuities between legacy and digital-first media forms. Such an understanding can usefully problematise overly rigid distinctions between 'traditional' and 'digital' media (Turner 2016) and significantly expand the conceptual and analytical boundaries of 'food television'. Yet there is also something about online food videos that escapes any reading of these texts as simply (or primarily) televisual. In fact, while Google's strategy of making YouTube "more like TV" has contributed to the proliferation of online content that mirrors many legacy television conventions, it has also led to the production of texts that possess an affective power that must be understood in its own specificity.

Eating affect

If the user were to click on the link to MetDaan's 'These cakes are called PERFECTION', they would be taken to the full videos on Rosie's Dessert Spot, an Australian-based YouTube channel (547K subscribers) featuring elaborate cake-decorating tutorials. The turquoise drip cake and rainbow ice-cream cake that featured in my Facebook news feed appear as two separate tutorials on Rosie's Dessert Spot: 'How to Make an Easy Loaded Upside Down Drip Cake' (10.7K views) and 'How To Create An Ice-Cream Themed Cake' (23K views). Each video contains step-by-step methods, integrated product recommendations, and Rosie's easy-to-follow instructional commentary. The tutorial for the turquoise drip cake begins with instructions for cutting the cake, sandwiching the layers with buttercream, applying the crumb coat, applying and smoothing the outer frosting layer, creating the drip effect, and adding the final decorations. The tutorial for the rainbow ice-cream cake offers instructions for applying the crumb coat, making two cake tiers, creating the ombre effect, preparing the decorations, and creating the melted ice-cream 'look'. Each step is demonstrated visually and explained via commentary, with additional tips and suggestions at key moments (for example, how to prevent the drips running too far down the cake or how to ensure visual balance in the decorations). The video, like most Rosie's Dessert Spot tutorials, concludes with Rosie encouraging viewers to try the cake themselves and to tag her on social media with the results.

With their focus on clear instruction and encouragements to 'try this at home', elements of Rosie's videos do indeed appear to apply the pedagogical conventions of earlier televisual genres to an online context shaped by increased expectations of interaction between creators and users. Rosie herself would also be at home on much mainstream food television. With her youthful good looks, she exemplifies the white, middle-class bodily norms so often a precondition for success in both online content creation and mainstream media (Duffy 2017: 103). But while baking channels like Rosie's Dessert Spot preserve recognisable links with conventional forms of food television, they also adopt a range of additional conventions that exceed the pedagogical and lifestyle functions of these earlier media forms.

For example, like many other YouTube baking channels, Rosie's Dessert Spot dispenses with the direct address expected of food television (and replicated by more 'mainstream' channels like Nerdy Nummies), centring the cake (rather than the host) as the visual focus. In most of Rosie's videos, only her hands and torso are visible. Food television's conventional address to camera is replaced by a post-production voice-over, outlining each step. At first glance, such conventions would seem to enhance the videos' didactic and pedagogical functions, offering explicit verbal instruction and a visual emphasis on the cake to assist the viewer in replicating the recipe at home. Indeed, the fact that Rosie maintains a side business selling the cake-decorating equipment she uses on her channel suggests that a sufficient portion of her audience does indeed attempt to make her recipes themselves. But as the viewer watches Rosie's disembodied hands form beautifully decorated cakes and listens to the sound of her soothing, softly spoken voice, these videos (like those of the content aggregators that remediate them) simultaneously produce an excess of affect that cannot be understood simply in terms of instruction or even aspirational lifestyle. Much like the online videos enjoyed by Evans (2016) and Greenberg (2016), the digital affordances of Rosie's Dessert Spot can also be seen to tap into the affective comforts of baking and the visceral pleasures of watching food we need not ever make or eat.

These affective sensations can produce embodied experiences that blur the lines between the material and the virtual. In their analysis of Tasty's short-form food videos, Schlussel and Frosh (2020) show how, despite the appearance of instruction, the simplicity and intimacy of online food content gives rise to "hyper-sensory" experiences that prioritise embodied, affective engagement over informational use or narrative involvement. They show how the videos' semiotic, interactive, and haptic qualities combine to produce tactile experiences that engage the user's senses, rather than serving informational purposes. In particular, they argue, online food videos often blur the distinction between touch and vision. For example, filming hands preparing food at a high angle, in ways that approximate the user's own point of view if he or she were preparing the food, produces a visual continuity between the hands depicted on screen and the user's hands holding their electronic device (Schlussel & Frosh 2020). Users' haptic interactions with digital interfaces (swiping, scrolling, etc.) work to further situate the viewer in embodied encounters with the video content.

This blurring of the distinction between touch and vision has also been observed by Anna Lavis (2017), whose work on pro-ana (pro-anorexia) communities has revealed how engagements with online food can profoundly disrupt conventional understandings of food and eating. Lavis' participants described their online encounters with digital food media (photos, videos, and the like) not as experiences of *vicarious* consumption (e.g. Adema 2000) but as akin to *actual* ingestion, generating feelings of satiety, guilt, or nausea. Participants described viewing food media to satisfy cravings for 'forbidden' foods, sometimes until they felt sick: "like I ate too much", as one participant put it (Lavis 2017: 203). Digital media environments, Lavis argues, can thus produce powerful visceral (as opposed to simply 'virtual') experiences that can give rise to "nascent and contingent forms of eating", in which eating itself becomes reconfigured and retextured (Lavis 2017: 198). While pro-ana communities represent a highly specific (and extreme) enactment of online eating, the participants' engagements with digital food nonetheless highlight the necessity of moving beyond paradigms of eating as something involving only corporeal mouths and stomachs, understanding it instead as something that can also take place in (and assemble) brains, eyes, and digital screens, in simultaneously embodied and disembodied encounters (Lavis 2017: 201). This materiality of the virtual collapses neat distinctions between on- and off-line worlds. "[E]ating on the Internet", Lavis writes "remaps vectors of ingestion and digestion beyond individual or bounded biologies. In doing so, it … draw[s] … into view not only the virtuality of the material, but also the materiality of the virtual" (Lavis 2017: 203).

If digital food media can give rise to nascent and contingent forms of eating, as Lavis (2017: 198) suggests, then it may equally be possible that online food videos can give rise to nascent and contingent forms of *cooking*. The user may, for example, imagine Rosie's hands as their own, as they skilfully create a flawless cake. The identificatory logic is further amplified by the short-form videos (such as Tasty's) that present anonymous, on-screen hands as an extension of the viewer's own, inviting the user into an embodied experience of vicariously preparing the food. For example, a recent Tasty video that begins with a recipe for a mirror-glaze cake, 'Mesmerizing Desserts for A Dinner Party' (158K views), offers the viewer the point of view of the cook: it positions the viewer as if it is their own hands preparing the layers of cake, jam, and white chocolate mousse and finishing the cake with a gleaming, bright red glaze. Even for those with no intention of replicating the dinner-party desserts, the videos may nonetheless offer the pleasures of cooking's visual and haptic sensations—without the labour, mess, or risk of failure they would likely experience in the off-line world.

As Deborah Lupton (2019: 151) has pointed out in a slightly different context, food is invested with vital capacities that enhance or diminish bodily affects, as well as contributing to the enactment of micro- and macro-political relations that cannot always be anticipated in advance—even in the seemingly ordinary and quotidian content of online food videos (such as a layer cake tutorial). Lupton's research applied a feminist materialist analysis to a range of food photos, videos, GIFs, and memes, to show how digital food content incites intensities and affective forces that can have variously progressive and reactionary ends. These forces can work to generate positive forms of belonging and activism (for example, within vegan or fat acceptance communities) or to maintain unequal social relations (for example, in the case of masculine online communities defined through the often violent consumption of meat). Lupton (2019: 152) shows how digital food media can shape the construction of individual identities and broader political orientations, creating "vital forces and agential capacities for feeling, learning or action". The "vitalities and visceralities" of digital food media are linked to the specific content of media texts, but also exceed the representational logics of these texts. They thereby engender affective forces that can generate, shape, and order actions and interactions between human and non-human actors, and bring these to the attention of digital media's often very large audiences (Lupton 2019: 151, 165).

Digital food media's 'vital capacities' explain in part the affective states of relaxation and calm that commentators attribute to online food videos. Tasty frames its content in both instructional and affective terms. Its taglines, "Snack-sized videos and recipes you'll want to try" and "Food that'll make you close your eyes, lean back, and whisper 'yessss'", simultaneously invoke the pragmatic pleasures of learning new dishes and a wordless bliss that exceeds mere practical mastery. The titles of videos often reflect their dual purpose. 'Mesmerizing Desserts for A Dinner Party', for example, highlights both the practical application of recipe techniques (i.e. ideas for desserts one might actually prepare for a dinner party) and the affective state being generated by the experience of viewing (i.e. the state of being mesmerised). Indeed, if such videos can arguably give rise to nascent and contingent forms of cooking, then the use of extreme close-ups and time-lapse video serve further to amplify the materiality and tactility of the food. In 'Mesmerizing Desserts for A Dinner Party', this includes ultra-close-ups of soaking gelatine (with time lapse to highlight the dramatic change in texture), of thick ganache straining through a sieve (filmed from both low and high angles to generate visceral sensations of movement), and of waves of mirror glaze being poured onto the cake in repetitious circular motions (and in quantities beyond those strictly required to achieve the glaze effect). These serve to elicit tactile, physical sensations—"hyper-sensory" experiences (Schlussel & Frosh 2020)—that place the viewer *in* the video.

Rosie's Dessert Spot treads a similar line between the practical and the blissful. Her videos for the upside-down turquoise drip cake and the rainbow ice-cream cake provide enough information that the viewer *could* recreate the recipes themselves. But the speed and skill with which Rosie prepares the cakes give rise to unique pleasures of their own. In contrast to the boisterous cheerfulness of hosts like Pansino, Rosie's softly spoken voice-over includes no filler or instruction beyond what is essential, allowing the viewer to focus on the mesmerising spin of the cake turntables as the finished cakes are revealed. These affects are perhaps further amplified in the videos' silent remediation via MetDaan Cakes, where not even Rosie's gentle commentary intrudes on the videos' hypnotic visual pleasures. Indeed, the fact that none of Rosie's viewers appears to have tagged her in a reproduction of either recipe suggests that actually making these cakes may not be a central motivation for many users. Scrolling through the comments beneath the videos, it is clear that some subscribers do indeed follow Rosie's Dessert Spot for practical decorating ideas and advice (e.g. "You've just given me an idea for my sisters [sic] birthday cake. I'm definitely trying this"). But a sizeable number of commenters also remark on the visual pleasures of Rosie's creations and the soothing nature of her voice (e.g. "Beautiful voice and decorations"; "Your voice is sooo soothing... and i love all your decorations...").

Autonomous sensory meridian responses

In many respects, the soothing affects generated by Rosie's Dessert Spot and other food videos are similar to those of ASMR (Autonomous Sensory Meridian Response). ASMR is a niche but increasingly popular genre of online videos designed to produce 'tingling' physiological responses and states of relaxation through the use of audio and visual triggers. ASMR videos come in a variety of forms, the most popular focusing on the minutiae and acoustic textures of mundane domestic activities, such as towel folding, table setting, and ironing (Gallagher 2016). Such videos are often explicitly framed as relaxation and sleep aids (Anderson 2015: 686), with their mixing and recording techniques designed to create an illusion of hyper-proximity through which viewers can feel, and be soothed by, the material intimacies of sounds (Gallagher 2016). In many of the scenarios, a fixed camera and microphone stand in for the viewer's head as they are directly addressed by the ASMR artist, who uses audio and visual triggers (including whispering, crinkling, and popping) to invoke embodied sensations of physical touch, such as the feeling of one's hair being brushed or face stroked (Gallagher 2016; Hudelson 2020: 196; Smith & Snider 2019: 42). These "digital intimacies" often centre around gendered notions of care, with the most popular of these helping, soothing, or reassuring scenarios presented by women performing as "benignly solicitous figure[s]" (Gallagher 2016; see also Smith & Snider 2019: 45).

While clearly entangled in gendered notions of care and emotional labour (Hudelson 2020: 194)—something perhaps equally true of the feminised world of online baking—the capacity of ASMR to create feelings of proximity, tactility, and comfort highlights the way mundane sounds can serve as a mechanism for material and affective experiences (Smith & Snider 2019: 41). In the rapidly growing genre of ASMR-inspired cooking and baking videos, these typically dispense with the 'classic' ASMR whispering and focus instead on the vitalities and visceralities of food as their key sources of affect. In such cases, the videos focus less on experiences of solicitation and service and instead locate the viewer *in* the videos through sounds and images that invoke affective experiences of relaxation, comfort, or indulgence. For example, Cooking Tree—perhaps the most popular ASMR baking channel on YouTube, with nearly 4M subscribers—combines high-quality video with augmented audio designed to play upon the cultural connotations of baking as comfort. With no voice-over and the host's face never shown, Cooking Tree videos focus on the gentle, meditative actions of stirring, sifting, whipping, and assembling. Any potentially distressing sounds (such as the noise of electric beaters) are pleasantly muted. The videos combine relaxation and instruction in a soothing, predictable format: each video first introduces the dish (to a background of gentle piano muzak) before the ingredients list is shown in English and Korean; the dish is then prepared, with on-screen captions outlining the step-by-step method; and, finally, the finished dish is shown being portioned and served for eating.

Although the clear ingredients lists and instructions suggest that Cooking Tree videos invite viewers to replicate the recipes shown, the cooking methods are presented in a surplus of detail that heightens the videos' visual and sonic materiality. For example, the Pastel

Rainbow Crepe Cake (one of the channel's most popular recipes, with 10.5M views) lingers on each step of the recipe far longer than is necessary for purely instructional purposes. The video shows the careful and methodical preparation of the crepe mixture (combining the eggs, sugar, and flour; straining the batter into a jug; transforming its appearance with food colouring), cooking all ten crepes in five different colours (rather than just one or two to demonstrate the process), carefully layering the crepes with whipped cream on the spinning cake turntable, and piping flawless rosettes of cream on the top.

Through each of these steps we see only the host's hands, mostly shot from a high angle. As in Tasty videos, this camera position gives the viewer the point of view of the cook. The final two minutes or so of each video is generally spent preparing and portioning the dessert for eating. In the case of the rainbow crepe cake, we see cut slices revealing the perfect rainbow layers followed by a fork cutting pieces of cake as if to be eaten. Although some videos include crunching and chewing sounds, the viewer never sees the host actually eating the finished dessert. Instead, as each mouthful is loaded onto the fork, it is brought towards the camera as if to the viewer's mouth. Such textual techniques invite the viewer to go beyond mere 'watching' of the content on screen, and instead to position themselves materially *within* the video as both cook and eater.

Such videos capitalise on a range of digital affordances (in particular, the accessibility of high quality at-home recording technologies; platform interfaces and algorithms that bring particular kinds of content to the attention of users; and the haptic and sensory relations between users and personal screen devices) to reframe mediated forms of food and cooking not so much as sites of representation (i.e. as something to be *watched*) but as generating affects that invite immersive and visceral engagements. The videos do this through their amplification of food's materiality: heightened, hyper-proximate sounds of flour being sifted or cream being whipped; soothing pastel colours; and tantalising images and sounds of consumption. The visual and aural pleasures of these videos may not elicit the 'tingling' feeling of conventional ASMR, but if the commentary surrounding them is any indication (see Lee 2020), they do give rise to feelings of comfort, relaxation, and calm—much as baking itself is popularly understood to do (Grande 2020).

As Rob Gallagher (2016) has argued of ASMR more generally, these videos can be seen as a reflection of the "growing importance of networked devices as means of self-medicating with media, of creating 'bubbles' of pleasure, solace, concentration or belonging". The deliberately heightened materiality of ASMR videos attunes us to the ways in which texts are not simply made up of meanings, but also of visual and sonic triggers that (to paraphrase Lavis 2017: 198) can bring together texts, platforms, and bodies in encounters that 'retexture' both cooking and eating to produce new cultural forms and experiences of affect. This need not be limited to ASMR but can also include other texts capable of producing "bubbles of pleasure, solace, concentration or belonging", from Rosie's soothing voice gently narrating the steps of a successful cake decoration, to the hypnotic, silent spinning of the cake turntables in videos by Tasty or MetDaan Cakes.

Affect switches

In such contexts, Brodmerkel and Carah's (2016) concept of "affect switches" offers a potentially useful framework for understanding the significance of the sonic and visual materiality of online food videos and the affective states they elicit. The concept of "affect switches" comes from their work on contemporary advertising, which, they argue, has increasingly shifted away from a reliance on persuasive or symbolic claims (for example, about the quality or meaning of a product) towards the development of branded objects and architectures that seek to modulate people's behaviour through the generation of affects (Brodmerkel & Carah 2016: xiv). In *Brand Machines, Sensory Media and Calculative Culture*, they argue that contemporary brands have essentially become 'brand machines' that coordinate the interplay between cultural and computational processes and orchestrate networks of generative relationships by switching and stimulating the transfer of affect.

Brodmerkel and Carah give the example of Heineken's 2013 promotion, which was designed to augment the experience of nightclubs. The promotion used 'smart' beer bottles that would flash in specific rhythms or patterns in response to the proximity of other bottles or to the music being played by the DJ. The bottles constituted an 'affect switch' in the sense that they worked to integrate Heineken beer into the rhythms of light, sound, and interaction that clubs stimulate, and, in turn, implicated participating consumers in affective relations involving humans, branded objects, and media systems. As Brodmerkel and Carah (2016: 105, 107) put it:

> [T]he bottle [is] not only a container for the product, or even ... a symbolic device that carries a brand logo on its label, but rather ... an I/O [input/output] device that stores and transmits information

Affect switches: Affective capture and market logics 79

between living bodies and media platforms ... The bottle is an affect switch that senses sound and movement, transforming it into flashes of light that prompt consumers to interact with each other, capture images and circulate them as part of their enjoyment of nightlife.

The example of smart bottles shows how brand machines create touch points between living bodies and computational media systems, seeking to produce bodily affects, nudge bodies in a certain direction, or stimulate and intensify their attention (Brodmerkel & Carah 2016: 105). For Brodmerkel and Carah (2016: 103) the affect switch generally constitutes a branded, Internet-of-Things material object. But the concept is sufficiently broad to include any object, physical or virtual, that stimulates the body of the consumer and provides a transfer point between living bodies and media systems.

Consequently, if we recognise YouTube's and Facebook's commercial, algorithmic logics as constituting both brand machines and calculative media systems, it becomes possible to argue that their practices (much like Heineken's smart bottles) may equally operate as affect switches that engage bodies and platforms in simultaneously affective and calculative encounters. The affect switches of online cooking and baking videos, for example, can "stimulate ... and channel ... the transfer of affect" via transfer points between bodies, data, and media systems (see Brodmerkel & Carah 2016: 100). Affective states of relaxation and comfort can be achieved through the haptic activities of swiping and scrolling, which often serve to produce a visual continuity between the viewer's hands and those on screen, as well as through the video's visual and aural materialities, which 'touch' the viewer through sound and movement: the spinning cake turntables, the oozing ganache, the squelching of eggs and gelatine as they mix into the batter.

But these material touch points also bring bodies and data into the service of the algorithmic and market rationalities of digital platforms, in much the same way as the Netflix competition shows discussed in Chapter 2. In the case of online food videos, the visual and aural materialities of platform content produce forms of engagement to be translated into data (analytics, algorithms, etc.) for investment in the maintenance of platforms' own brand value and to generate further data for calculation. YouTube and Facebook depend for their success not only on the calculation of users, whose viewing habits shape, and are shaped by, platform algorithms, but also the calculation of creators, whose own calculative encounters with platform architectures generate opportunities for increased visibility, engagement, and (potentially) monetisation (Bishop 2018; Gerhards 2019). Indeed, for those content creators and genres best able to capitalise on market opportunities, affect switches can serve both their own and the platform's generative capacities as brand machines. To borrow a phrase from scholars of ASMR, the significance—and brand value—of online food videos perhaps lies less in their messages, to be understood or interpreted, and more in their ability to elicit affective and somatic 'outputs' that enable units of sensation to be exchanged for units of attention (Gallagher 2016; see also Hudelson 2020: 195). Jessica Maddox (2021) characterises these units of exchange as "transactional tingles", through which relaxation for the viewer is exchanged for metrics (e.g. likes, views, comments) that lead to potential monetisation and for the capacity to shape future videos and the algorithmic systems that organise online content.

If, as Brodmerkel and Carah (2016: 111) argue, the power of affect switches lies in their capacity to "enable new configurations of audience attention, affect and action" to be sold to advertisers, then online food videos are especially generative of marketing, branding, and advertising opportunities. The genre has appealed enormously to advertisers, who have capitalised on opportunities for sponsored videos and product placements (Gerhards 2019), as well as more conventional forms of advertising that exploit the affective states generated within the videos. For example, both Tasty and Rosie's Dessert Spot adopt product placement strategies well-honed by earlier forms of food television, combining in-video product placements with product links in the videos' description boxes, connecting the positive associations generated by the videos with products ranging from baking equipment to Nestlé chocolate. For channels like Cooking Tree, where the main revenue generators are pop-up ads and interstitial spot advertising, food's affective capacities to enable "new configurations of audience attention, affect and action" (Brodmerkel & Carah 2016: 111) give rise to opportunities for advertising techniques that adopt and replicate many of the material triggers used within the videos. For example, while conducting the research for this chapter, Cooking Tree videos were regularly punctuated by Cadbury Crunchie's "Kick It To The Crunchie Beat" ad, using amplified sounds of crunching honeycomb and crackling wrappers to create a hip-hop beat in ways that not only mimicked sounds in Cooking Tree videos but also reflected the rise of ASMR techniques in conventional advertising more broadly (Johnson 2019).

As Chapter 2 argued, digital food TV's economic models increasingly depend on the (invisible and uncompensated) labour of television

Affect switches: Affective capture and market logics 81

personalities and audiences. Online baking videos highlight the additional role of affective states in shaping platform brands, the content they house, and the data they generate. As Gallagher (2016) has put it, in a slightly different context, online food videos highlight the "affective dynamics and algorithmic underpinnings of consumer capitalism in an era when ... markets are increasingly governed by 'sensual logic' rather than rationality". While food's vitalities and visceralities may produce affects that cannot simply be reduced to commercial logics, the videos' "transactional tingles" may be ideally suited to turn affective excess into calculable ends. Transactional tingles can assemble bodies, platforms, and experiences in ways that—for content producers like Tasty or MetDaan Cakes—capitalise on the seamless interplay between their own marketing systems and Facebook's architecture (Brodmerkel & Carah 2016: 110), allowing them to locate commercial logics in everyday moments, such as eating breakfast. For channels such as Rosie's Dessert Spot or Cooking Tree, the generative capacities of affective experiences provide avenues for financial compensation for content creators, but also loosen creators' control over the meanings and uses these affects serve. In such cases, the encounters between bodies and calculative media systems contribute to strategies for monetisation that privilege external brand logics, and the sonic and visual triggers originally used for purposes of instruction, pleasure, or relaxation are adopted and replicated for quite different ends.

As Brodmerkel and Carah (2016: 176) point out, the critical issue is not so much that digital platforms are saturated with branded content, but rather that the protocols, interfaces, and algorithms of the platforms themselves are often specifically designed to manage and enhance brand value. Brodmerkel and Carah's study of contemporary brand culture demonstrates that the analysis of brands is fundamentally political. They argue:

> [A]n analysis of the brand – if it is to be politically charged as regulation, activism or everyday resistance – must grapple with the interface between our bodies and their lived experience in the computational infrastructure of media.
>
> (Brodmerkel & Carah 2016: 184)

Understanding the interface between bodies and computational media systems is not just essential to an analysis of brands, however. It is also essential to the analysis of digital platforms and the content they circulate, promote, and (de-)prioritise. This is especially important given that the majority of diverse content on digital platforms can effectively be obscured by algorithms that prioritise good visual and audio quality, noncontroversial content, white middle-class content creators, and videos that can be matched easily with branded tie-ins (Bishop 2018: 72).

The vitalities and visceralities of online food

A properly political analysis of online food videos, then, necessitates understanding not just the everyday uses to which such videos are put, but also the new modes of being and action that these media make visible, configure, and affect (or not). It must also seek to understand not just the political power of everyday practices or the algorithmic data that underpin and shape the interactions between bodies and calculative media systems, but also the political potential of food media's affects. This chapter has shown how online food videos' "vitalities and visceralities" (Lupton 2019: 151) exceed the apparently instructional function of digital food texts, producing nascent and contingent forms of cooking and eating that are simultaneously virtual and material. The affects of online food videos may not be produced simply in the service of commercial logics, but they can be readily captured and (re) directed by them, making the "affective capacities of bodies available to the information processing power of platforms" (Dobson, Carah & Robards 2018: 20).

Such outcomes highlight that, even in the digital realm, food politics is always a visceral politics (Hayes-Conroy & Hayes-Conroy 2013). Understanding food politics in this way helps us to see everyday embodied practices and affective relationships as processes "in and through which broader political economic forces take shape and are constituted" (Hayes-Conroy & Hayes-Conroy 2013: 88). In the realm of online food videos, this kind of approach requires attention to the ways in which the reverberations and "affective fabrics of digital cultures" (Kuntsman 2012: 1)—that is, both platform interfaces and the content the platforms house and circulate—work with broader political and economic forces. Given that the most successful content creators in the baking genre are highly marketable, conventionally feminine women, it would be relatively straightforward to read the political forces underpinning online baking videos as primarily normative: seamlessly inserted into a commercial logic invested in reinforcing—and profiting from—conventionally gendered notions of baking and femininity (Nathanson 2015). But this chapter has also highlighted the extent to which online food texts possess an affective surplus that potentially escapes such simple readings. As I have shown, digital food media can materialise food's vitalities and visceralities in virtual spaces—and, in the process, retexture food and cooking in ways that generate embodied experiences that need not be read as exclusively available to feminine subject positions.

Indeed, to consider online food videos beyond their representational or instructional logics potentially allows us to expand the parameters of what cooking is, what is means, where and how it occurs, and in what ways it can be viscerally felt. Food affects can be shoe-horned into a calculative resource for financial accumulation—as they so often are in online food videos—but they also contain a political potential in their ability to enhance or diminish a body's capacity to act. We might ask: what "current habits of bodily (re)action" (Hayes-Conroy & Hayes-Conroy 2013: 84) could be interrupted or reimagined if digital food media's affects opened up new ways of thinking about what cooking is, what it means, and where it takes place? What currently unforeseen capacities (bodily or otherwise) could such thinking open up? Such questions take us quite far from our initial investigations into the instructional (or otherwise) role of digital food TV. But they nonetheless highlight ways in which we might redefine our understanding of the potentialities of the televisual and how the "forces, vibrancies and intensities" of digital media are generative of texts' political e/affects (Lupton 2019: 154), in ways that are not always obvious from their manifest content. As this chapter has shown, these potentialities may be especially available to food content that is native to digital platforms. However, as the following and final chapter suggests, digital affordances can also play a role in (re)shaping the politics of more traditional forms of food TV.

References

Adema, Paula 2000, 'Vicarious consumption: Food, television and the ambiguity of modernity', *Journal of American & Comparative Cultures*, vol. 23, no. 3, pp. 113–123. https://doi.org/10.1111/j.1537-4726.2000.2303_113.x

Anderson, Joceline 2015, 'Now you've got the shiveries: Affect, intimacy, and the ASMR whisper community', *Television & New Media*, vol. 16, no. 8, pp. 683–700. https://doi.org/10.1177/1527476414556184

Ashley, Bob, Hollows, Joanne, Jones, Steve & Taylor, Ben 2004, *Food and Cultural Studies*. Routledge: London.

Bishop, Sophie 2018, 'Anxiety, panic and self-optimization: Inequalities and the YouTube algorithm', *Convergence: The International Journal of Research into New Media Technologies*, vol. 24, no. 1, pp. 69–84. https://doi.org/10.1177/1354856517736978

Brodmerkel, Sven & Carah, Nicholas 2016, *Brand Machines, Sensory Media and Calculative Culture*. Palgrave Macmillan: London.

Burgess, Jean & Green, Joshua 2018, *YouTube: Online Video and Participatory Culture*. Polity: Cambridge.

Cooper, Jenny 2015, 'Cooking trends among millennials: Welcome to the digital kitchen', *Think with Google*, June, https://www.thinkwithgoogle.com/intl/en-gb/future-of-marketing/digital-transformation/cooking-trends-among-millennials/. Accessed 14 January 2022.

Couldry, Nick 2004, 'Theorising media as practice', *Social Semiotics*, vol. 14, no. 2, pp. 115–132. https://doi.org/10.1080/1035033042000238295

Cunningham, Stuart & Craig, David 2019, *Social Media Entertainment: The New Intersection of Hollywood and Silicon Valley*. New York University Press: New York.

Cunningham, Stuart, Craig, David & Silver, Jon 2016, 'YouTube, multichannel networks and the accelerated evolution of the new screen ecology', *Convergence: The International Journal of Research into New Media Technologies*, vol. 24, no. 4, pp. 376–391. https://doi.org/10.1177/1354856516641620

Dobson, Amy Shields, Carah, Nicholas & Robards, Brady 2018, 'Digital intimate publics and social media: Towards theorising public lives on private platforms'. In Amy Shields Dobson, Brady Robards & Nicholas Carah (eds), *Digital Intimate Publics and Social Media*. Springer: Cham, pp. 3–27.

Duffy, Brooke Erin 2017, *(Not) Getting Paid to Do What You Love: Gender, Social Media, and Aspirational Work*. Yale University Press: New Haven, CT & London.

Evans, Dayna 2016, 'Why these recipe videos are taking over your Facebook wall', *The Cut*, 23 March, http://www.thecut.com/2016/03/zen-and-the-art-of-the-buzzfeed-tasty-video.html. Accessed 14 January 2022.

Gallagher, Rob 2016, 'Eliciting euphoria online: The aesthetics of "ASMR" video culture', *Film Criticism*, vol. 40, no. 2. https://doi.org/10.3998/fc.13761232.0040.202

Gerhards, Claudia 2019, 'Product placement on YouTube: An explorative study on YouTube creators' experiences with advertisers', *Convergence: The International Journal of Research into New Media Technologies*, vol. 25, no. 3, pp. 516–533. https://doi.org/10.1177/1354856517736977

Grande, Laura 2020, 'Why we're drawn to comfort baking in times of stress', *Food Network Insider*, 21 November, https://www.foodnetwork.ca/food-network-insider/blog/comfort-baking-stress-psychologist/. Accessed 14 January 2022.

Greenberg, Julia 2016, 'Food has eaten the Internet and it tastes like a vampire taco', *Wired*, 30 May, https://www.wired.com/2016/05/internet-reached-perfection-looks-like-vampire-taco/. Accessed 14 January 2022.

Hayes-Conroy, Jessica & Hayes-Conroy, Allison 2013, 'Veggies and visceralities: A political ecology of food and feeling', *Emotion, Space and Society*, vol. 6, pp. 81–90. https://doi.org/10.1016/j.emospa.2011.11.003

Hudelson, Joshua 2020, 'Wages for soundwork: ASMR as reproductive labor', *Resonance: The Journal of Sound and Culture*, vol. 1, no. 2, pp. 191–210. https://doi.org/10.1525/res.2020.1.2.191

Johnson, Lauren 2019, 'Millions of Americans just learned what ASMR is from Michelob Ultra's Super Bowl commercial—but they aren't loving it', *Business Insider*, 4 February, https://www.businessinsider.com/michelob-ultras-asmr-super-bowl-commercial-2019-2019-2?r=AU&IR=T. Accessed 14 January 2022.

Kirkwood, Katherine 2018, 'Integrating digital media into everyday culinary practices', *Communication Research and Practice*, vol. 4, no. 3, pp. 277–290. https://doi.org/10.1080/22041451.2018.1451210

Kuntsman, Adi 2012, 'Introduction: Affective fabrics of digital cultures'. In Athina Karatzogianni & Adi Kuntsman (eds), *Digital Cultures and the Politics of Emotion: Feelings, Affect and Technological Change*. Palgrave Macmillan: London, pp. 1–17.

Lavis, Anna 2017, 'Food porn, pro-anorexia and the viscerality of virtual affect: Exploring eating in cyberspace', *Geoforum*, vol. 84, pp. 198–205. https://doi.org/10.1016/j.geoforum.2015.05.014

Lee, Jolin 2020, 'Wake and bake calmly with these ASMR baking channels on YouTube', *Lifestyle Asia*, 17 April, https://www.lifestyleasia.com/kl/culture/entertainment/asmr-baking-channels-youtube/. Accessed 14 January 2022.

Lewis, Tania 2020, *Digital Food: From Paddock to Platform*. Bloomsbury Academic: London.

Lobato, Ramon 2016, 'The cultural logic of digital intermediaries: YouTube multichannel networks', *Convergence: The International Journal of Research into New Media Technologies*, vol. 22, no. 4, pp. 348–360. https://doi.org/10.1177/1354856516641628

Lupton, Deborah 2019, 'Vitalities and visceralities: Alternative body/food politics in digital media'. In Michelle Phillipov & Katherine Kirkwood (eds), *Alternative Food Politics: From the Margins to the Mainstream*. Routledge: London, pp. 151–168.

Lupton, Deborah 2020, 'Carnivalesque food videos: Excess, gender and affect on YouTube'. In Deborah Lupton & Zeena Feldman (eds), *Digital Food Cultures*. Routledge: Abingdon, pp. 35–49.

Maddox, Jessica 2021, 'What do creators and viewers owe each other? Microcelebrity, reciprocity, and transactional tingles in the ASMR YouTube community', *First Monday*, vol. 26, no. 1. https://doi.org/10.5210/fm.v26i1.10804

Marwick, Alice E. 2016, 'You may know me from YouTube: (Micro-)celebrity in social media'. In P. David Marshall & Sean Redmond (eds), *A Companion to Celebrity*. Wiley Blackwell: Chichester, pp. 333–350.

Morley, David 2009, 'For a materialist, non–media-centric media studies', *Television & New Media*, vol. 10, no. 1, pp. 114–116. https://doi.org/10.1177/1527476408327173

Nathanson, Elizabeth 2015, 'Sweet sisterhood: Cupcakes as sites of feminized consumption and production'. In Elana Levine (ed.), *Cupcakes, Pinterest, and Ladyporn: Feminised Popular Culture in the Early Twenty-First Century*. University of Illinois Press: Urbana-Champaign, pp. 249–267.

Patel, Sahil 2016, 'With Facebook video, the aggregators are winning', *Digiday*, 28 April, https://digiday.com/media/facebook-video-aggregators-winning/. Accessed 14 January 2022.

Schlussel, Hadas & Frosh, Paul 2020, '"Taste this video!" Facebook videos as embodied experiences', *Selected Papers of #AoIR2020: The 21st of Annual Conference of the Association of Internet Researchers*, 27–31 October. https://doi.org/10.5210/spir.v2020i0.11326

Smith, Naomi & Snider, Anne-Marie 2019, 'ASMR, affect and digitally-mediated intimacy', *Emotion, Space and Society*, vol. 30, pp. 41–48. https://doi.org/10.1016/j.emospa.2018.11.002

Strange, Niki 1998, 'Perform, educate, entertain: Ingredients of the cookery programme genre'. In Christine Geraghty & David Lusted (eds), *The Television Studies Book*. London: Arnold, pp. 301–312.

Strangelove, Michael 2010, *Watching YouTube: Extraordinary Videos by Ordinary People*. University of Toronto Press: Toronto.

Think with Google 2016, 'Baking on YouTube—How niche communities provide huge opportunities for marketers', *Think with Google*, December, https://www.thinkwithgoogle.com/intl/en-cee/future-of-marketing/digital-transformation/baking-youtube-how-niche-communities-provide-huge-opportunities-marketers/. Accessed 14 January 2022.

Turner, Graeme 2016, *Re-inventing the Media*. Routledge: London.

van Dijck, José 2013, *The Culture of Connectivity: A Critical History of Social Media*. Oxford University Press: Oxford.

4 Technologies of intimacy
Reimagining broadcast food TV in the pandemic

So far, this book has understood digital food TV primarily in terms of content produced for and/or distributed on digital platforms. The aesthetic conventions and industrial logics of digital TV depart in some significant ways from those of the broadcast and cable television industries that dominated earlier food television scholarship. This distinction between 'digital' and 'legacy' TV is largely artificial, of course, since both broadcast and cable TV have been 'digital' for quite some time. But it has nonetheless been useful for interrogating the specific politics and affects of contemporary televisual industries and their role in shaping the cultural place of food in a digital era. This final chapter, however, departs from the book's primary focus on digitally distributed food content, to consider ways in which 'traditional' television is also shaped by textual conventions and production techniques derived from digital platforms. In particular, the chapter focuses on the changes to broadcast television that occurred during the COVID-19 pandemic. As audiences (re)turned to the medium in record numbers (Hermes & Hill 2020), the pandemic prompted a surge in demand for new television content while necessitating the adoption of production strategies compliant with stay-at-home and social distancing measures.

These changes occurred across a range of broadcast television genres, most notably exemplified by the Zoom interviews and virtual 'studio' audiences that have been a recurring feature of news, current affairs, and talk programs since early 2020. This chapter focuses on the changes occurring in broadcast food television, particularly in the programs of established celebrity chefs. Although some celebrity chefs, deprived of their professional studios and media crews at the height of the pandemic, sought to engage their audiences via social media (particularly YouTube, Facebook, Instagram, and TikTok), others refocused on the traditional mass audiences of broadcast output.

DOI: 10.4324/9781003261940-5

88 Technologies of intimacy

The latter group included Jamie Oliver who, early in the pandemic, released his made-for-Channel-4 cooking program, *Keep Cooking and Carry On*; the show was subsequently broadcast on streaming, free-to-air, and cable networks in the UK, Australia, New Zealand, North America, Europe, and the Middle East. The 20-episode series, produced on a smaller budget than usual for Oliver's cooking programs, and more hastily pulled together, was billed as offering 'flexible' recipes that viewers could adapt to their own circumstances and ingredient availability—as stay-at-home orders in the UK and elsewhere disrupted supply chains and emptied supermarket shelves of fresh fruit and vegetables, eggs, meat, and pantry staples (Sharman, Sawer & Newey 2020). *Keep Cooking and Carry On* began as a professionally produced program, but once harsher lockdown restrictions made it impossible for Oliver to continue filming in his studio kitchen, the final 14 episodes were filmed in Oliver's home on his mobile phone.

This chapter explores the ways in which the shift to at-home filming disrupted the traditional logics and aesthetics of celebrity-led food television, in ways that (for a moment, at least) suggested new possibilities for reimagining the contemporary cultural role of food and food television. The ways in which these possibilities were (and were not) realised highlight how food TV's politics are now often highly contingent and provisional—while nonetheless revealing the medium's (often unpredictable) 'moments of possibility' and emergence. I argue that the mobile recording technologies and domestic location of *Keep Cooking and Carry On* offered digitally produced feelings of intimacy and connection, generating what Misha Kavka (2014: 461) would call a 'cusp formation'—an interface or join that emerges from media's ability to connect people across distances and enables new possibilities to emerge. The chapter shows how this cusp was generated through *Keep Cooking*'s 'low-tech' production style, the feelings of access and immediacy that this produced, and its disruption of the smooth narrative and visual flow typical of broadcast lifestyle cookery programs. While *Keep Cooking* depicts a lifestyle that is out of reach for most viewers, the cusp produced by its seemingly amateurish production worked to connect viewers with Oliver and each other, in a version of what John Ellis (1982: 136–137) would call 'co-presence': an experience of being together rather than simply 'watching' from the outside. At a time when many around the world were confined to their homes, this worked to frame domestic spaces not only as sites of meaning and action during the pandemic but also as sources of digital intimacy and community that could extend beyond the privatised space of the family home. *Keep Cooking and Carry On*, then, points to the significant potential of digital food TV to generate affective engagements that can enable a rethinking (at least temporarily) of the traditional relationships between private and public spaces, celebrities and ordinary people, food and cooking, and the role of the televisual in mediating these.

The capacity of *Keep Cooking*'s digital production techniques to enable a cusp formation can be seen especially clearly when the show is considered in relation to its follow-up program, *Easy Meals for Every Day*. *Easy Meals* went to air not long after *Keep Cooking* concluded, but the difference between the two programs could not have been more stark. While *Easy Meals* was also filmed in Oliver's home, the easing of COVID restrictions in the UK meant that the show could be filmed with an on-site camera crew and production staff. The return to professional production saw the abandonment of *Keep Cooking*'s digital techniques, in favour of a more polished style that replaced the earlier show's seemingly spontaneous approach with carefully stage-managed, 'lifestylised' representations of Oliver family life. As a result, the opportunities that *Keep Cooking* offered to reimagine television's domesticity and domestication during COVID-19 were effectively closed down, as *Easy Meals* reframed the family home not as a potential site of connection and community but instead as a space of retreat. Nonetheless, there was a moment in which *Keep Cooking* suggested that things could be different, revealing the potential for digital food TV's production practices and techniques to generate new meanings and affects, as I explore in this chapter.

Intimate television

While the circumstances of the pandemic may have intensified audience experiences of television as an "intimate screen" (Jacobs 2000; see also Leppert 2020), especially by granting us increased access to celebrities' homes, television had been understood as a medium of intimacy long before COVID-19 restrictions. Television's history as a popular medium, its formative years shaped by post-war expansion of the domestic sphere and the 'domesticity' of its own subject matter (Hartley 1998; Spigel 1992), has meant that intimacy—and domestic intimacy, in particular—has long been understood as a specifically televisual mode. In an influential early formulation, Horace Newcomb (1974) argued that one of television's signature achievements is its capacity to bring characters and personalities directly into people's homes—a feature that has not just persisted, but intensified, as television has matured as a medium (Newcomb 2008: 30). Television's

90 *Technologies of intimacy*

ability to grant domestically located viewers unique forms of access to other people is especially relevant to lifestyle and reality TV, in which large numbers of 'ordinary' people have shared intimate details of their lives as participants on programs ranging from health to appearance to parenting (Skeggs & Wood 2009). The "direct, intimate personal" modes of address that have long been understood as a hallmark of television (Scannel: 1996 12) have been central to the construction of food and lifestyle personalities, where the expertise of the television celebrity is presented in 'ordinary', accessible, and inclusive ways (Bell & Hollows 2005: 15).

This has resulted in television food personalities "feel[ing] like trusted friends" whom we know intimately (Johnston & Goodman 2015: 205). This sense of connection is central to the success of food celebrities like Nigella Lawson, whose camp, conspiratorial address invites viewers to feel as though they are getting a peek into her home, her private dinner parties, and surreptitious midnight snacks (Lawson 2009). Feelings of personal connection are also central to the success of Jamie Oliver, as Tania Lewis (2008: 13) describes:

> Lifestyle experts are comforting, neighbourly figures whom we feel we 'know' on a first-name basis—Jamie [Oliver] and Martha [Stewart] being classic exemplars of this—familiar faces who regularly pop up on our screens ... giving us various 'how-to' tips for our everyday lives, people who, in their emphasis on their own role as homemakers, wives, husbands, and parents 'like us', feature almost as an extension of our friendship network.

Indeed, Oliver appears regularly in food TV scholarship as an example of reality and lifestyle television's turn to 'ordinary' forms of expertise (Lewis 2008). While Oliver's actual expertise comes from his training as a professional chef, his television persona seeks to democratise this specialist knowledge through his much-maligned "mockney" accent and "Essex-boy patter in which food is 'pukka' and 'wicked'" (Ashley et al. 2004: 175), presenting cooking as fun and accessible to all.

Oliver's longevity as a television personality has meant that viewers have watched him 'grow up' on screen, transforming from the young, carefree bachelor of *The Naked Chef* to the more responsible family man of recent years. The strong "parasocial relationships" that Oliver has maintained with his audience (Piper 2015: 253) stem in no small part from television's capacity to spark and sustain mediated intimacies. As Kavka (2014: 468) puts it, television's history as a "domestic, familial, and familiarising medium" means that its "promise ... to bring people *close*" is central to its affective potential (emphasis in original). Television's technologies of closeness and intimacy invite viewers to invest in Oliver's family, with his children and wife Jools regularly appearing on screen. Indeed, audiences' identification with Oliver's perceived normality as a cook and family man has been key to sustaining his success as a food celebrity (Piper 2015).

However, audiences' feelings of familiarity with food and lifestyle television hosts exist in tension with the out-of-reach lifestyles of many of the genre's most well-known personalities. Critics have noted, for example, the extent to which Oliver's earlier shows, like *The Naked Chef*, feel as much like lifestyle advertising as cookery programs (Ashley et al. 2004: 176; Moseley 2001: 39): Oliver's chic London apartment and regular outings to Soho's specialist food shops appear at odds with the show's otherwise democratic, "anyone can do it" messaging. Oliver's cooking shows, then, offer an example of the tensions between the 'ordinary' and the 'aspirational' that exist on food and lifestyle television: perceived feelings of ordinariness, closeness, or intimacy between audiences and television personalities potentially obscure the ways in which such programming can be designed to serve decidedly *un*ordinary commercial and aspirational ambitions.

This is, in part, why some scholars have argued that the intimacy and ordinariness once thought to be television's defining characteristics are now better achieved via newer digital technologies, the ubiquity, privacy, and domesticity of which work to re-construct television's intimate screen for a digital age (Creeber 2011: 592; see also Couldry 2004: 355; Levine 2008: 406). Such thinking has contributed to growing scholarly interest in the new intimacies afforded by the digital, including social media platforms (Dobson, Robards & Carah 2018; Hjorth & Arnold 2013), online video (Creeber 2011), and livestreaming (Ruberg & Lark 2021). Nonetheless, it is worth revisiting broadcast television's role as a technology of intimacy, especially in the context of the COVID-19 pandemic, during which television producers increasingly adopted mobile and digital recording techniques within more traditional broadcast contexts. In broadcast food television, these trends combined to reframe (at least temporarily) not just what food television 'is', but also how it works, politically and affectively. These potentialities and their limits are especially evident in Oliver's cooking shows from this time, particularly *Keep Cooking and Carry On*, which went to air approximately one month after the pandemic was officially declared in March 2020.

Keep Cooking and Carry On

The first episode of *Keep Cooking and Carry On* begins with a direct-to-camera address in which Oliver tells the audience:

> So we're living in unprecedented times of change, everything's changing day by day. And I wanted to respond to you guys quickly to give you a program that was relevant. And what does that mean? It means I need to give you recipes that are flexible—truly flexible—allowing you to swap things in and out ... so no matter what, I can give you the best chance to get decent grub on the plate and feed yourself and the people that you love ... So, guys: we can do this. We can absolutely do this. Let's get cooking and let's have a go.

Repeated references to "flexibility", "we can do this", and (later) "we're all in this together" and "let's lift the spirits" appear as refrains throughout the series. Oliver's opening address, like the series itself, does not explicitly mention the pandemic, but frames it euphemistically in terms of "unprecedented times" and "times of change". Key to Oliver's attempt to engage audiences appears to be his informal mode of address to viewers as "guys" and "we", which seeks to frame the challenges of the pandemic as stemming from a shared sense of collective experience.

Despite this seemingly egalitarian mode of address, however, an almost aggressively didactic undertone permeates the series' first few episodes. Recipes become opportunities to impart messages that reflect Jonatan Leer's (2017: 23) observation that Oliver "seems to take a more and more patriarchal position" in each program in which he participates. When cleaning up after preparing raw chicken for a curry, Oliver's reminder to viewers to "keep washing" their hands clearly relates implicitly to more than just food preparation. When telling viewers that they can easily substitute leeks for onions in a veggie chilli recipe, Oliver says, rather exasperatedly: "We can swap these things out, guys. No problem. Let's be flexible". There is a clear implication that it is not only in cooking that Oliver feels greater flexibility is needed: as Joanne Hollows (2022: 160) notes, Oliver's repeated calls for 'flexibility' reveal how, even in a pandemic, "people were still required to exhibit the qualities of the good neoliberal citizen". Other recipes are peppered with messages about the importance of cooking as a means of looking after oneself and loved ones, in ways that (implicitly and explicitly) link home-cooked food with positive health outcomes. This is especially clear in episode 2, when Oliver says to the audience, while preparing a salad recipe:

> The idea of getting salad into your life, or veggies, I think is really important right now. Having a balanced diet and having optimum health at the moment for a really good immune system is truly important.

The corollary—that a failure to cook or to "get ... salad into your life" reflects a failure to take adequate responsibility for one's health—is implied (see Hollows 2022: 162), but never explicitly stated. Nonetheless, the show's messaging reflects similar tactics to Oliver's earlier campaigning culinary documentaries, which often placed the onus on consumers to protect their health through individual dietary 'choices' (Gibson & Dempsey 2015).

As Jessica Martin (2021: 358) has argued, *Keep Cooking and Carry On*, with its emphasis on individual responsibility and its intertextual references to British wartime propaganda, was just one of a number of celebrity-led media texts that assisted in normalising and amplifying the "patriotic stoicism and nationalistic sentiment" of the UK government's own messaging during the early days of COVID-19. (Kirstie Allsop's television program *Keep Crafting and Carry On* is noted as another key example.) For Martin, the discourses of personal responsibility and "austerity nostalgia" (Potter & Westall 2013: 159) that permeate such programs ultimately worked to silence critique of the inequalities wrought by the pandemic. She suggests that such programs—and their celebrity hosts, whose wealth and privilege enabled them to insulate themselves from the worst impacts of the pandemic—were (and remain) complicit in the government's "duplicitous reassertions that we are 'all in this together'", as well as its framing of essential workers as "heroes" who need to keep up the fight (rather than exploited labourers who deserve pay rises and safe working conditions) (Martin 2021: 362). Indeed, Oliver's offer, in the closing credits, of "big love to those on the frontline in the NHS and essential services" and his unrelenting 'can do' tone throughout the earlier episodes not only lend the program the feel of a public service announcement: they also construct the audience as an undifferentiated 'we', in which everyone is in an equal position to do their part to battle the pandemic, whether by working heroically on the "frontline" or "staying at home" to stop the spread.

The failure to acknowledge the myriad constraints on people's ability to stay at home—or to prepare home-cooked meals—was typical of celebritised media culture during the early days of the pandemic (Kay 2020; Martin 2021). On the early episodes of *Keep Cooking*, any differences in experience are glossed over with persistent discourses of 'flexibility', revealing the extent to which the show's austerity messaging centred not so much on economic constraint but the absence of choice: "the inability for middle-class consumers to choose what to eat when they wanted it" (Hollows 2022: 161). However, it is notable that, while 'flexibility' is presented as a moral necessity for those watching at home, very little of Oliver's own cooking seems to require any modification. At the level of ingredient choice, for example, Oliver has (apparently) ready access to multicoloured vegetables, a range of fresh herbs, and ample rice and pasta—far more characteristic of the aesthetic conventions of his pre-pandemic lifestyle food programs than of the restricted access to ingredients faced by many Britons (and those elsewhere in the world) at the time of broadcast. In this respect, *Keep Cooking* exemplifies how food television's aestheticised, "lifestyled" (Lewis 2008: 6) conventions may not necessarily translate well into more didactic, public service formats—a critique that has also been levelled at other Oliver programs (such as *Jamie's Food Revolution*), which tend to take middle-class norms and values as their starting point and do not adequately recognise inequalities of class, income, or access to fresh food (Gibson & Dempsey 2015). For similar reasons, analysis of a show like *Keep Cooking and Carry On* must maintain a critical view of the hierarchies produced by the framing of staying (and cooking) at home as unquestioned moral and civic duties—notwithstanding that doing so (if one can) may indeed help to save lives (Kay 2020; Martin 2021).

Drawing viewers close

Once Oliver moved to at-home filming, however, *Keep Cooking* revealed a potential for mediatised narratives of 'home' to construct a different role for television—and food—during the pandemic. While the shift to at-home filming did not entirely overcome the problems of the show's overall 'stay at home' messaging, it did suggest possibilities that cannot be straightforwardly reduced to the critiques levelled at the studio episodes. As I will argue, central to *Keep Cooking*'s affective charge is its capacity to generate the feelings of intimacy and closeness that Kavka (2014) posits as essential to television's operation as a cusp formation. Compared with the polish and ease of the studio episodes, the at-home filming appears far more amateurish and shambolic. Filmed in the empty larder of Oliver's 16th-century country house, and relying solely on the in-built cameras and microphones of the Oliver family's mobile phones, shots are often poorly lit and clumsily framed, and the sound is frequently echoey and muffled. Unless Oliver's wife Jools or their children were on hand to help with filming, Oliver was limited to a single fixed camera, and hence to addressing his audience from a static position. Even when a second mobile phone was used to allow multi-angle shooting, limitations to the cameras' movement and range necessitated close-up focus on Oliver for most of the filming.

Such constraints lend the episodes a stripped-back, almost low-tech, feel that capitalises on the affective intimacy of the close-up (Ellis 1982: 130, 131). Indeed, the mobile phone's truncated field of view means that Oliver's face is often more of a focus than the food he is cooking. We see the lines and wrinkles around his eyes and on his hands. Without professional lighting and make-up, he often appears visibly tired. He is often unshaven. His hair is dishevelled. He cooks in pyjamas, bare feet, and (sometimes) torn clothes. Without access to the abundant and aesthetically pleasing array of ingredients he had in the studio kitchen, he cooks with limp and sad-looking carrots, makes do with odds and ends of vegetables, and makes a small amount of rice go further by bulking it out with noodles. He burns the food and keeps cooking. He cooks one recipe with food on his sleeve. He cooks another with food on his face. The kids come in and interrupt. We frequently hear his youngest son River playing—and sometimes screaming—out of shot.

This chaotic, amateurish feel is enabled largely by the portable, high-tech capabilities of contemporary mobile recording technologies, the affordances of which would have been unthinkable even a few years ago. Affectively speaking, however, the use of these technologies in a broadcast television context feels deceptively *low*-tech, and this adds to the sense of intimacy and immediacy in these episodes. By filming recipes in what appears to be a single take—with interruptions and mistakes left in, as they occurred—*Keep Cooking* draws viewers *close*, in Kavka's (2014: 468) terms, producing what feels like a real-time window into Oliver's preparation of daily family meals. These feelings of closeness and "constructed unmediation" (Kavka 2008: 7, emphasis removed) are reinforced by the brief footage that concludes each recipe of the Oliver family eating lunch or dinner. Although Oliver's identity as a family man has long been central to his food celebrity, and his family members regularly appear on screen, the family footage in *Keep Cooking and Carry On* is distinctly different from the tightly controlled, highly lifestylised glimpses into his family life that pepper his other television programs. Shot selfie-style from Oliver's phone camera, the family footage is often badly framed and lit, and the children shriek, make jokes, and seem completely unselfconscious in the camera's presence. Unlike the staged family meals and other festivities in Oliver's pre-pandemic programs—requiring hours of set-up, careful positioning of camera, lighting, and sound equipment, and proper screen and sound testing—the camera phone's portability and informality lend the footage the feel of a private family video, rather than something produced with a national and international broadcast in mind.

If, as Kavka (2014: 469) has suggested, television (and reality television, in particular) is a technology of intimacy in which the medium's mobilisation of closeness and proximity is crucial to its affects, then part of *Keep Cooking and Carry On*'s closeness is literal—given the ways in which the camera's limited movement and highly truncated field of view necessitate a close-up focus on Oliver. But part of the show's closeness is also the immediacy and access generated by the single takes, limited editing, regular interruptions, and imperfect presentation: each of these helps to situate the viewer *within* the televisual world, rather than as an outsider looking in. In other words, such techniques lend the footage an intimacy, as if "events are somehow *co-present with the viewer*, rather than witnessed from outside" (Ellis 1982: 136–137, emphasis added).

Certainly, social media comments on *Keep Cooking and Carry On* suggests that this is how some audiences, at least, engaged with the content. Tweets using the #KeepCookingCarryOn hashtag frequently commented on the 'normality' and 'naturalness' of Oliver's family; many of those posting stated that watching the show made them feel like they were right there "in [Oliver's] kitchen" or were "part of [Oliver's] family", indicating feelings of parasocial connection. That said, although the production conventions may indeed have lent the program a sense of immediacy and access, this does not mean that choices were not deliberately made—nor that the footage provides an unmediated window into Oliver's family life. There is nothing 'natural', for example, about Oliver's dishevelled appearance: he could have brushed his hair, changed out of his pyjamas, or re-shot footage to present himself in a more flattering light. Equally, additional takes or post-production editing could have removed three-year-old River's on-screen interruptions and off-screen tantrums. The footage we see is, in fact, most likely the result of deliberate choices designed to present Oliver as an ordinary middle-class dad trying to balance work, family, and cooking during the pandemic. Such strategies are part of how his message that "we're all in this together" is mobilised, visually and discursively, and how the Oliver family's circumstances are presented as relevant and relatable to those (middle-class viewers, at least) watching at home.

Indeed, the Oliver family's apparent 'relatability' is a key part of how the show works to elide inequalities and silence critique. As Jilly Boyce Kay (2020: 883, 884) warns, we must be wary of the resurgence of "mystificatory images of the heteronormative private household" that appeared during COVID-19, particularly the carefully curated images of 'ordinary' domesticity offered by celebrities. Kay (2020: 884) gives Arnold Schwarzenegger's stay-at-home video—filmed in his large kitchen where he feeds carrots to his pet pony and donkey—as an example of celebrity culture's disingenuous expressions of solidarity with 'ordinary' people. And, certainly, there are obvious, similar critiques to be made of Oliver's own privilege, his ability to choose to stay at home, and the comfort in which he is able to do so: he and his family self-isolated in a £6 million mansion boasting 9 bedrooms, 10 bathrooms and 70 acres of land (Best 2021). There are also obvious critiques to be made of the unchallenged heteronormativity of the Oliver family household, with its clear gendered division of labour: Jamie may be responsible for everyday family meals, but it is Jools who is shown hanging out the washing, mopping the floor, and overseeing care of the children.

But unlike the Schwarzenegger video, which shows the actor's kitchen and dining room in ways that feel obviously staged and where it is impossible to ignore the absurd opulence of a donkey and pony living in the house, *Keep Cooking and Carry On* plays with (in)visibility, closeness, and their affects in ways that potentially trouble any straightforward reading of its textual content. As Kavka (2008: 7, 156) argues (and as I suggested in Chapter 3), television's affects cannot always be immediately 'read off' the ideological content of its texts. Instead, through its technologies of intimacy, television can also give rise to affective responses that may exceed any controlled meaning-production. Kavka theorises television's affects as a cusp formation in which the screen amplifies feelings of proximity and co-presence, linking viewers and on-screen participants in an "indeterminate space of possibility that enlivens and enlarges the formulaic mechanisms of television production" and creates new points of emergence and potential (Kavka 2014: 461).

In Kavka's (2014: 469) understanding of affect, proximity is crucial to a body's potential to affect and be affected, and the technologies of television production are especially well suited for mobilising closeness. On *Keep Cooking and Carry On*, proximity is produced by the specific affordances and constraints of the mobile phone camera, but it is also produced by bringing into public view some of the intimacies of the Oliver household that would normally have been kept private, or at least carefully managed before being produced for public dissemination. The home video footage of family meals, the children's tantrums and interruptions, and Jamie's and Jools' on-camera appearances without studio wardrobe and make-up all bring essentially private moments into public view in ways that are atypical of the Olivers' other television appearances. They work to grant the viewer access to aspects of Oliver family life that feel unusually intimate—but the apparent 'closeness' also works to keep things *out* of view that would otherwise draw attention to the inequalities between Oliver and his audience. A brief camera pan during a recipe may offer a millisecond's glimpse out the window to the courtyards and outbuildings of the property's extensive grounds. The larder's open doorway may hint at a more expansive house on the other side of the threshold. But although the Oliver family does indeed live in an enormously expensive mansion, the limited field of view of the mobile phone camera gives viewers only the briefest glimpse of their out-of-reach lifestyle. The lack of professional cameras and lighting makes the rooms we do see feel small and dark. The effect—when combined with the spontaneous eruptions from River, our access to other 'personal' moments in Oliver family life, and the less polished mode of delivery—is an intimacy and immediacy produced by an excess of visibility (on the one hand) and persistent *in*visibility (on the other).

A cynical reading might conclude that this interplay between visibility and invisibility serves to universalise Oliver's circumstances in ways that make his message to "keep cooking and carry on" less open to critique. In other words, the show reveals enough to enable viewers to identify with the apparent 'normality' of Oliver's family but does not reveal *so* much as to highlight the significant gulf between Oliver's privileged situation and the more ordinary circumstances of his audience. Certainly, this critique of the show cannot be ignored. At the same time, however, an alternative reading might reveal the ways in which the show's techniques of drawing viewers physically and affectively close highlight television's capacity to "undo social distancing" (Hermes & Hill 2020) in ways not necessarily tied to Oliver's specific circumstances and privileges. As Joke Hermes and Annette Hill (2020: 658, 659) argue, television has the capacity to provide feelings of "throwntogetherness" that allow audiences to take imaginary part in the lives of others. This capacity, Hermes and Hill (2020: 659) suggest, was amplified under lockdowns, when television was "re-consolidated ... as master storyteller and as platform for cultural citizenship" and redefined as "a space in which to think about, reflect on and (re)form identities that are embedded in communities of different kinds, both existing in real life and virtually". Hermes and Hill use the 'Olive and Mabel' videos, filmed by BBC sports presenter Andrew Cotter, to exemplify not only how television production was impacted by the pandemic, but also the unique capacity of the televisual to bring together demographically and geographically dispersed audiences over shared interests and concerns (2020: 656).

We can also see in pandemic television a shift in the relationship between on- and off-screen personalities, with celebrities and public figures increasingly beaming into our homes from their own domestic spaces, and reliance on video calling making many people's 'ordinary' lives look more and more like television (Leppert 2020: 497, 498). Indeed, it could be argued that many of the images occupying our screens during this period—images similar in quality to Oliver's presentation on *Keep Cooking and Carry On*—functioned to reduce some of the visual distinctions between celebrities and ordinary people in media and public spaces. This softening of previously distinct boundaries not only amplified opportunities for audiences to take imaginary part in the lives of others: it also increased the potential for certain types of television programming to function according to Kavka's (2014) cusp formation, in which the screen is understood as a join or membrane that connects physically distant others and enables new possibilities to emerge. The identificatory relationships with Oliver that *Keep Cooking* invites highlight the ways in which the cusp formation is indeterminate (Kavka 2014: 461) and not necessarily straightforwardly progressive. The flattening of distinctions between celebrities and ordinary people can (in under some conditions) work to reduce hierarchies, but it can also insulate from critique the structures of privilege and inequality that make celebrity—and television production itself—possible, by inviting audiences to imagine that Oliver and his family are "just like us".

Yet by drawing viewers close, *Keep Cooking and Carry On* also offered other, more positive, possibilities. These stem not so much from viewers' access to apparently 'real' aspects of Oliver family life, or even from the fact that many middle-class viewers may have been able to recognise aspects of their own life in Oliver's experience (although both may have been true). Rather, they stem from the ways in which the show's filming techniques and modes of address worked to construct a bridge or connection between on-screen personalities and those watching at home, as well as between viewers themselves.

This provides another example of how food's mediated, affective experiences can expand the parameters of what cooking is, what it means, and where and how it occurs. In the case of *Keep Cooking*, such experiences were affirmed and amplified via the show's dialogic elements: the just-in-time nature of production allowed Oliver to respond quickly to audience needs and enabled audiences to 'speak back' to Oliver and each other. *Keep Cooking*'s recipes often responded explicitly to audience requests (via Oliver's website and social media channels) for advice on substituting ingredients subject to shortage. For instance, viewers might ask what to make if they couldn't find dried pasta, or how to adapt recipes to shortages of rice, bread, or other ingredients. This, in turn, allowed viewers to respond to Jamie, and to other audience members, in more collaborative ways than is typical of Oliver's 'regular' television cooking shows—sharing their own recipes to use up leftovers or surplus ingredients, or using the #KeepCookingCarryOn hashtag to offer their own ingredient swaps for Oliver's dishes in cases of specialised or hard-to-find ingredients (substituting ginger orange marmalade for tamarind in his eggplant curry, for example).

Online audiences also revealed the capacity of *Keep Cooking*'s recipes to traverse a greater range of cooking relationships and spaces than the normative, domestic family cookery depicted in the show itself. For example, several audience posts to Twitter included photos of primary-school-aged children preparing recipes from the show as gifts for single or elderly neighbours. Another post showed children of NHS workers cooking Oliver's flapjack recipe with childcare staff. A woman from Victoria, Australia, posted a photo of herself cooking one of Oliver's recipes next to a computer screen showing her Tasmanian-based nephew preparing the same recipe alongside. In all these cases, the recipes from *Keep Cooking and Carry On* are shown as offering sources of connection not only within the privatised space of the family home, but also extending beyond it. That is, audiences' responses to Oliver's recipes revealed the ways in which dishes initially designed as inspiration for individualised, 'private' households could become, though mediation, sources of connection for a wider range of communities and relationships.

Such responses to *Keep Cooking*, then, suggest a moment in which the program's didactic tendencies and inherent inequalities were—or, at least, could be—partially disrupted. Audience posts presented cooking as a source of neighbourly connection, a means of supporting essential workers and social justice organisations, and a tool to connect geographically distant family members across generations. In doing so, these posts offer the home not as a private, apolitical realm: rather, public mediation can flow both to and from the home, and the connections it generates can be experienced both physically and virtually. Thus, such posts suggest possibilities for reimagining the home—and home cooking—as spaces from which to rethink how public and private lives can be constructed, conducted, and made meaningful. These posts also highlight the capacities of food television to reconfigure relationships between public and domestic spheres in ways that can alter how the politics of these spheres can emerge and be mobilised. Indeed, the specific potential of *Keep Cooking*'s technologies of intimacy to give rise to this sort of reimagining becomes especially clear once we consider Oliver's subsequent program, *Easy Meals for Every Day*—in which the adoption of a more polished, professional style worked essentially to close the cusp that *Keep Cooking* had partially opened.

Easy Meals for Every Day

With its professional camera crew, sound technicians, and hair and make-up artists, *Easy Meals for Every Day* saw a return to the 'lifestylisation' that has long been a hallmark of Oliver's cookery programs. Abandoning the mobile phone camera and its truncated field of vision, *Easy Meals* opens with an establishing shot of Oliver's enormous two-storey country house. Tightly framed, the shot nonetheless reveals (as far as the viewer can tell) at least five upstairs bedrooms, plus a large downstairs area surrounded by a vast lawn. The effect is to bring into full view aspects of the Olivers' home that had been invisible (or only partially visible) on *Keep Cooking*, and to reveal beyond a doubt the full extent of the wealth only hinted at in the earlier program. The episode then immediately cuts to Oliver, who is shown in a direct address to camera from the same larder in which *Keep Cooking* was filmed. He says:

> Like most of you in the last few months, I have had more time cooking at home for my family than ever before, using the ingredients we love in totally different ways to create simple, exciting and affordable meals.

As in *Keep Cooking*, the communal mode of address ("like most of you") suggests connection and commonality between Oliver and his audience. The larder—now professionally styled and lit—is bright, airy, and filled with chic, colour-coordinated knickknacks and kitchen equipment. We can now see the space fully, in contrast to *Keep*

Cooking, where our vision was partially obscured. Yet our enhanced visual access to Oliver's home has paradoxical effects: rather than drawing viewers close, the increased visibility highlights the distance between this space and the rather dingy, echoey room it seemed on *Keep Cooking and Carry On*—and, in turn, the distance between this space and the far less stylish domestic spaces in which "most of [us]" actually cook.

The distance between Oliver and his audience extends further once Oliver begins cooking. The show's recipes take place either outdoors in Oliver's garden or inside in a specially converted outbuilding that Oliver euphemistically describes as his "culinary potting shed". Oliver's is no ordinary garden, however, but rather a massive walled garden bursting with lush vegetable beds and bordered by espaliered trees and manicured hedges. The "culinary potting shed" is a fully stocked, full-service kitchen with top-end appliances and shelves heaving with colourful, artfully arranged preserves, dried herbs, onions, and chillies. *Easy Meals* still includes occasional tears and tantrums— including one scene where River, dressed in a tutu and devil's horns, bursts into tears because the food is not yet ready—but, for the most part, Oliver family life no longer erupts in the seemingly spontaneous way of *Keep Cooking*. Instead, family appearances are carefully controlled and stage-managed, the unpredictable shrieks and hijinks of *Keep Cooking* replaced by serene family meals featuring clean and well-behaved children in colour coordinated outfits. The perfect weather and B-roll footage of green countryside, ladybirds, and summer wildflowers further add to the idyllism.

As a result, *Easy Meals* appears less a tool to assist audiences to manage mealtimes during the pandemic and more a peek into the wealth and privilege of Oliver family life. *Easy Meals* thus largely undoes *Keep Cooking*'s potential to reimagine the meaning and politics of home cooking. Discourses of 'making do' are still present in *Easy Meals*, but (as in the studio episodes of *Keep Cooking*) Oliver himself is no longer subject to any of the restrictions faced by (at least some of) his audience. With access to aesthetically pleasing heirloom vegetables, and few or no restrictions on staples, 'making do' in the Oliver household is largely limited to compromises like making prawns go further by bulking out kebabs with bread (artisan sourdough, of course!), while "mak[ing] use of what [they have] ... to hand" means cooking with their generous crops of homegrown vegetables.

Rather than opening up a cusp, then, *Easy Meals* instead provides a classic example of the aspirational logic of lifestyle television, whereby the home—and the country home, in particular—is constructed as a place of fulfilment, plenitude, and escape from the pressures of day-to-day urban life (Phillipov 2016). If *Keep Cooking* revealed the affective and political possibilities that can arise from the intimacy of only partially seeing, these possibilities were ultimately closed down once the true extent of the wealth and opulence of Oliver's lifestyle became visible. As a result, rather than offering the home as a space through which to reimagine and re-view how we understand relationships of care and affiliation, and the connections and intersections between public and private spaces, the Oliver family home is ultimately revealed to be (literally) walled off from the outside world—a barricade produced by high walls and financial prosperity. Not only does this work to construct the home as a site of privileged retreat, in ways warned against by Martin (2021: 360): the tightly controlled and stylised view also abandons the co-present intimacies of the earlier series in favour of broadcast food television's more conventional, aspirational logics (although not even the middle classes could recognise anything of their own lives here). As a result, viewers are no longer drawn close, but produced at a distance, and the capacity for food television to "undo ... social distancing" (Hermes & Hill 2020: 655) is itself undone.

Indeterminate affects

A show like *Keep Cooking and Carry On* can readily be critiqued for its representation of the family home as a privileged space of retreat during a global pandemic. But the digital intimacies it generated nonetheless highlight its capacity to produce a cusp formation distinct from more 'typical' celebrity-led, broadcast cookery programs. Ideologies of 'ordinariness' and 'authenticity' have long been central to the construction of food celebrity, but such ideologies have often sat at odds with the otherwise aspirational, middle-class logics of television production. This is certainly true of *Keep Cooking*, given that its production was made possible by the Oliver family's spacious and comfortable lockdown conditions, which most could only dream of. But by confining the field of view and drawing viewers close, the show's digital techniques also worked to remove from visibility the most out-of-reach trappings of Oliver family life, which were subsequently shown fully in *Easy Meals for Every Day*.

Rather than entrench distance between television and its audience, *Keep Cooking*—with its seemingly 'amateurish' production and dialogic engagement with audiences—revealed the capacity for affective feelings of proximity to construct the home as a portal for forms of connection and community both within and beyond the domestic sphere. As Kavka (2008: 37) puts it in a slightly different context:

> the TV screen is not a glass barrier between illusory and real worlds; instead, the screen is a join that amplifies affect and connects real people on one side with the real people, in another sense, on the other side.

As a domestic, reassuring, and familial medium, television has long had the capacity to draw viewers close. But in the mediatised aesthetics of COVID-19, in which the homes and domestic experiences of both celebrities and ordinary people were increasingly on public display, *Keep Cooking*'s digital intimacies hinted at the possibility that relationships between television and its audiences could be reconfigured (at least partially). This included a potential for reimagining, among other things, the role of celebrity and the televisual in times of crisis, the private sphere as a space in which to mediate public experiences (and vice versa), and the home—and home cooking—as conduits for new forms of outreach and political action. As Kay (2020: 883) argues, the intensified focus on the home during COVID-19 has the potential to entrench inequality further, but it also offers the possibility of re-visioning private spaces and their models of domesticity, kinship, and care beyond the private family.

In the case of *Keep Cooking*, the Oliver family's experience of pandemic life may be out of reach of the ordinary person, but the show's capacity to draw viewers close—both to on-screen personalities and other viewers—offers audiences the opportunity to identify not so much with the program's explicit content but with its *affects*. As I have suggested, these affects are not always or even necessarily politically progressive. But at the convergence of broadcast industries, digital techniques, and public and private spaces, there was a moment in which *Keep Cooking and Carry On* moved away from an aggressively didactic mode of address to a far more intimate, indeterminate one, that (temporarily at least) suggested more positive possibilities. By utilising the closeness fostered by TV in general and digital technologies in particular, *Keep Cooking* highlighted an opportunity for reimagining and rebuilding. However, the cusp that was partially opened was quickly closed by *Easy Meals for Every Day*, when production returned to highly aestheticised, aspirational depictions of food, cooking, and domestic life.

It is telling that this shift paralleled the broader cultural trend in which early commentaries that COVID-19 offered an opportunity to do capitalism differently (e.g. Mair 2020; Mazzucato 2020) were quickly abandoned as the pandemic progressed and 'normal' ways of doing and being in the world prevailed. Shows like *Keep Cooking and Easy Meals* reveal the political potentialities of digital food TV, but also its limits in advancing lasting change, particularly in more fully reimagining and "rebuild[ing]" (Kay 2020: 887) domestic spaces and practices. In variously mobilising and resisting the new forms of affective connection that arose from the public mediation of private spaces during the pandemic, broadcast food television during this time simultaneously hinted that a different sort of domestic politics may be possible and revealed the ease with which food and cooking can be repurposed for a range of (progressive and reactionary) political goals, with implications that were not always knowable in advance.

References

Ashley, Bob, Hollows, Joanne, Jones, Steve & Taylor, Ben 2004, *Food and Cultural Studies*. Routledge: London.
Bell, David & Hollows, Joanne (eds) 2005, *Ordinary Lifestyles: Popular Media, Consumption and Taste*. Open University Press: Maidenhead.
Best, Chloe 2021, 'Jamie Oliver and his wife Jools' £6million country estate is idyllic—see inside', *Hello!*, 7 September, https://www.hellomagazine.com/homes/gallery/20210510112771/jamie-oliver-jools-house-essex-inside-photos/1/. Accessed 14 January 2022.
Couldry, Nick 2004, 'Liveness, "reality", and the mediated habitus from television to the mobile phone', *The Communication Review*, vol. 7, no. 4, pp. 353–361. https://doi.org/10.1080/10714420490886952
Creeber, Glen 2011, 'It's not TV, it's online drama: The return of the intimate screen', *International Journal of Cultural Studies*, vol. 14, no. 6, pp. 591–606. https://doi.org/10.1177/1367877911402589
Dobson, Amy Shields, Robards, Brady & Carah, Nicholas (eds) 2018, *Digital Intimate Publics and Social Media*. Springer: Cham.
Ellis, John 1982, *Visible Fictions: Cinema, Television, Video*. Routledge & Kegan Paul: London.
Gibson, Kristina E. & Dempsey, Sarah E. 2015, 'Make good choices, kid: Biopolitics of children's bodies and school lunch reform in *Jamie Oliver's Food Revolution*', *Children's Geographies*, vol. 13, no. 1, pp. 44–58. https://doi.org/10.1080/14733285.2013.827875
Hartley, John 1998, 'Housing television: Textual traditions in TV and cultural studies'. In Christine Geraghty & David Lusted (eds), *The Television Studies Book*. London: Arnold, pp. 33–50.
Hermes, Joke & Hill, Annette 2020, 'Television's undoing of social distancing', *European Journal of Cultural Studies*, vol. 23, no. 4, pp. 655–661. https://doi.org/10.1177/1367549420927724

Hjorth, Larissa & Arnold, Michael 2013, *Online@AsiaPacific: Mobile, Social and Locative Media in the Asia-Pacific*. Routledge: London.

Hollows, Joanne 2022, *Celebrity Chefs, Food Media and the Politics of Eating*. Bloomsbury Academic: London.

Jacobs, Jason 2000, *The Intimate Screen: Early British Television Drama*. Clarendon Press: Oxford.

Johnston, Josée & Goodman, Michael K. 2015, 'Spectacular foodscapes: Food celebrities and the politics of lifestyle mediation in an age of inequality', *Food, Culture & Society*, vol. 18, no. 2, pp. 205–222. https://doi.org/10.2752/175174415X14180391604369

Kavka, Misha 2008, *Reality Television, Affect and Intimacy: Reality Matters*. Palgrave Macmillan: Houndmills.

Kavka, Misha 2014, 'A matter of feeling: Mediated affect in reality television'. In Laurie Ouellette (ed.), *A Companion to Reality Television*. Wiley Blackwell: Malden, pp. 459–477.

Kay, Jilly Boyce 2020, '"Stay the fuck at home!" Feminism, family and the private home in a time of coronavirus', *Feminist Media Studies*, vol. 20, no. 2, pp. 883–888. https://doi.org/10.1080/14680777.2020.1765293

Lawson, Jenny 2009, 'Food confessions: Disclosing the self through the performance of food', *M/C Journal*, vol. 12, no. 5. https://doi.org/10.5204/mcj.199

Leer, Jonathan 2017, 'Gender and food television: A transnational perspective on the gendered identities of televised celebrity chefs'. In Kathleen LeBesco & Peter Naccarato (eds), *The Bloomsbury Handbook of Food and Popular Culture*. Bloomsbury: London, pp. 13–26.

Leppert, Alice 2020, 'We're all television stars in a pandemic', *Celebrity Studies*, vol. 11, no. 4, pp. 496–499. https://doi.org/10.1080/19392397.2020.1834224

Levine, Elana 2008, 'Distinguishing television: The changing meanings of television liveness', *Media, Culture & Society*, vol. 30, no. 3, pp. 393–409. https://doi.org/10.1177/0163443708088794

Lewis, Tania 2008, *Smart Living: Lifestyle Media and Popular Expertise*. Peter Lang: New York.

Mair, Simon 2020, 'Could the huge shifts in our way of life being introduced as part of the fight against Covid-19 pave the way for a more humane economy?', *BBC Future*, 31 March, https://www.bbc.com/future/article/20200331-covid-19-how-will-the-coronavirus-change-the-world. Accessed 10 May 2022.

Martin, Jessica 2021, 'Keep crafting and carry on: Nostalgia and domestic cultures in the crisis', *European Journal of Cultural Studies*, vol. 24, no. 1, pp. 358–364. https://doi.org/10.1177/1367549420958718

Mazzucato, Mariana 2020, 'The Covid-19 crisis is a chance to do capitalism differently', *The Guardian*, 19 March, https://www.theguardian.com/commentisfree/2020/mar/18/the-covid-19-crisis-is-a-chance-to-do-capitalism-differently. Accessed 10 May 2022.

Moseley, Rachel 2001, '"Real lads do cook....but some things are still hard to talk about": The gendering of 8–9', *European Journal of Cultural Studies*, vol. 4, no. 1, pp. 32–39. https://doi.org/10.1177/136754940100400102

Newcomb, Horace 1974, *TV: The Most Popular Art*. Anchor Books: Garden City, NY.

Newcomb, Horace 2008, 'Reflections on *TV: The Most Popular Art*'. In Gary R. Edgerton & Brian G. Rose (eds), *Thinking Outside the Box: A Contemporary Television Genre Reader*. The University Press of Kentucky: Lexington, pp. 17–36.

Phillipov, Michelle 2016, 'Escaping to the country: Media, nostalgia, and the new food industries', *Popular Communication*, vol. 14, no. 2, pp. 111–122. https://doi.org/10.1080/15405702.2015.1084620

Piper, Nick 2015, 'Jamie Oliver and cultural intermediation', *Food, Culture & Society*, vol. 18, no. 2, pp. 245–264. https://doi.org/10.2752/175174415X14180391604288

Potter, Lucy & Westall, Claire 2013, 'Neoliberal Britain's austerity foodscape: Home economics, veg patch capitalism and culinary temporality', *New Formations*, vol. 80–81, pp. 155–178. https://www.muse.jhu.edu/article/529458.

Ruberg, Bonnie & Lark, Daniel 2021, 'Livestreaming from the bedroom: Performing intimacy through domestic space on Twitch', *Convergence: The International Journal of Research into New Media Technologies*, vol. 27, no. 3, pp. 679–695. https://doi.org/10.1177/1354856520978324

Scannell, Paddy 1996, *Radio, Television and Modern Life: A Phenomenological Approach*. Blackwell Publishing: Oxford.

Sharman, Laura, Sawer, Patrick & Newey, Sarah 2020, 'Supermarkets begin food rationing after wave of coronavirus-fuelled panic buying', *The Telegraph*, 7 March, https://www.telegraph.co.uk/news/2020/03/07/supermarkets-begin-food-rationing-wave-coronavirus-fueled-panic/. Accessed 14 January 2022.

Skeggs, Beverley & Wood, Helen 2009, 'The transformation of intimacy: Classed identities in the moral economy of reality television'. In Margaret Wetherell (ed.), *Identity in the 21st Century: New Trends in Changing Times*. Palgrave Macmillan: London, pp. 231–249.

Spigel, Lynn 1992, *Make Room for TV: Television and the Family Ideal in Postwar America*. University of Chicago Press: Chicago, IL.

Conclusion
Television and the politics of digital food

As the chapters in this book have shown, the landscape of contemporary digital food TV is shaped by the expansion in what constitutes 'food television'. New digital texts draw conventions from earlier cooking formats, older programs are reinvigorated through digital techniques, and both old and new food texts find new lives as digital platforms grow and expand. These developments have made food an especially generative case for exploring the textual, industrial, and infrastructural contexts underpinning the production of contemporary television and its relationship to the burgeoning digital content industries. And these developments reflect key changes to the cultural place of food and food media in a digital era, revealing "moments of possibility" (Barnes 2017) at the intersection of television's textual practices, platform logics, and market ideologies, as well as the new meanings, politics, and affects that are enabled and constrained by food TV's shift online.

Through studies of flow (Chapter 1), labour (Chapter 2), materiality (Chapter 3), and intimacy (Chapter 4), the chapters have revealed how digital food TV's meanings, politics, and affects are not always enacted in ways that our established assumptions and approaches have primed us to expect. Nor do they always appear in the places we have previously looked for them. Indeed, the distinct forms of flow produced by digital interfaces can work to disrupt our usual methods for interpreting the politics of digital food texts. With digital interfaces bringing together disparate texts in ways that evacuate them of their original historical and cultural contexts, the new forms of meaning-making these interfaces produce no longer necessitate reading texts in political terms—even for televisual genres like eco-reality, which have typically been understood as explicitly progressive in their messaging.

In the online databases of digital distribution, food television's politics is often no longer found in manifest messages or representations,

DOI: 10.4324/9781003261940-6

Conclusion 109

but in the ways that textual and platform practices give rise to affects that flatten or amplify intensity. For example, the flattening of intensity typical of streaming reality TV gives rise to affective experiences of comfort that assist in masking platforms' exploitative relationships with both contestants and audiences. Indeed, such experiences enable platforms to recast contestants' production and promotion labour as a form of leisure, in much the same way as the unpaid labour of audiences, whose own 'leisure' is essential to refining platform algorithms and infrastructures. This blurring of labour and leisure is also what helps to produce algorithmic alliances between food and other types of lifestyle content that similarly promotes highly flexible, individualised modes of self-entrepreneurship and exploitation as sources of pleasure.

It is food's affective excesses—its "vitalities and visceralities" (Lupton 2019: 151)—that makes it ideally suited to being re-purposed for calculative ends. As the discussion of online baking videos in Chapter 3 showed, such videos are not the primarily instructional texts they are often understood to be. They are, rather, sources of affective force and intensity that locate the viewer *in* the video in ways that expand the conceptual boundaries of food TV—and, indeed, what constitutes 'food' and 'cooking'. Such content creates touch points between bodies and calculative media systems that can move, extend, and capture bodies in various ways, including by bringing both bodies and data into the service of the algorithmic and market rationalities of digital platforms. But through their capacity to enhance or diminish a body's capacity to act, these videos also contain political potentials that can exceed market logics.

Digital food TV has the capacity to bring together texts, platforms, and bodies in encounters that can retexture food and cooking, their accepted meanings, and where and how these are thought to occur. As the example of *Keep Cooking and Carry On* illustrated, digital technologies can give rise to a cusp formation (Kavka 2014: 461) that can expand the spaces of food and cooking and the relationships and connections these enable. The manifest program content may have served to obscure and normalise Oliver's privilege to self-isolate comfortably during the COVID-19 pandemic, but the strategic play with visibility and invisibility afforded by the show's use of the mobile phone camera also offered a bridge beyond the privatised space of the Oliver family home—one that connected audiences with both Oliver and each other. Although the new imaginative and political potentialities this offered were only temporary, they nonetheless highlight the unexpected possibilities of emergence that can reside in the digital, the consequences of which are not always knowable in advance.

Conclusion

As a result, a more complete understanding of the changing and contingent politics of digital food TV necessitates a shift in the language of our critique. If the politics of digital food TV no longer lies primarily in the manifest textual content, but rather in the ways this content intersects with platform infrastructures and industrial and cultural contexts to produce momentary potential for possibility and rupture, then the ways we seek to identify or evaluate the politics of these texts also need to change. Specifically, we now need to advance critiques that preserve what Lavis (2017: 203) describes as the "uncertain, contingent and even … potential or anticipated … relationships that may arise among eating, foods, … bodies" and digital platforms.

While these relationships necessitate a new politics of food in a digital era, they also represent a politics 'beyond' food. If food offers a generative category for understanding contemporary transformations in television and digital content industries, it has also been a generative category for those industries themselves. Food has enabled such industries to form algorithmic connections with other areas of lifestyle, and to benefit from blurred boundaries between the playful, user-generated dimensions of online contexts and their increasingly dominant market logics. Food television's messages of pleasure and comfort have also allowed more insidious messaging—about neoliberal capitalism, for example, or contemporary labour relations—to go under the radar. As Ramon Lobato has put it (2018: 242), such complexities pose both new and old questions for television research. In the context of digital food, we need to continue to ask: what is food TV today? Where can it be located? What does it 'do'—culturally, politically, industrially?

This book has argued that, while these older questions remain relevant, and methods like textual analysis are crucial to our response, 'answers' can no longer be found in the explicit content of texts. Instead, the underlying question must be not so much about what is *represented*, but what is *imagined* by digital food TV. What is made possible (or impossible) in these imaginings? How can food TV's 'moments of possibility' alter the cultural and political work it now performs? As the case studies in *Digital Food TV* reveal, food television's cultural and political implications are now more contingent, more contextual, less obviously 'knowable' than they may have been previously. Understanding their full impacts necessitates attention to the complex intersections of textual representations, televisual production practices, and digital platform infrastructures which are shaping the meanings, politics, and affects that underpin the contemporary cultural place of food—and food media—in a digital era.

References

Barnes, Christine 2017, 'Mediating good food and moments of possibility with Jamie Oliver: Problematizing celebrity chefs as talking labels', *Geoforum*, vol. 84, pp. 169–178. https://doi.org/10.1016/j.geoforum.2014.09.004

Kavka, Misha 2014, 'A matter of feeling: Mediated affect in reality television'. In Laurie Ouellette (ed.), *A Companion to Reality Television*. Wiley Blackwell: Malden, pp. 459–477.

Lavis, Anna 2017, 'Food porn, pro-anorexia and the viscerality of virtual affect: Exploring eating in cyberspace', *Geoforum*, vol. 84, pp. 198–205. https://doi.org/10.1016/j.geoforum.2015.05.014

Lobato, Ramon 2018, 'Rethinking international TV flows research in the age of Netflix', *Television & New Media*, vol. 19, no. 3, pp. 241–256. https://doi.org/10.1177/1527476417708245

Lupton, Deborah 2019, 'Vitalities and visceralities: Alternative body/food politics in digital media'. In Michelle Phillipov & Katherine Kirkwood (eds), *Alternative Food Politics: From the Margins to the Mainstream*. Routledge: London, pp. 151–168.

Index

Note: Page numbers followed by "n" refer to end notes.

Adams, Jayde 42, 49
advertising: ASMR techniques 80; catch-up television 22, 34; and digital flow 20, 34–35; Facebook 65; influencing behaviour via affect generation 78, 80; lifestyle advertising 91; online food videos 80; reality television 48; traditional broadcast television 8, 20, 34
affect: affect switches 78–82; eating affect 71–75; triggers 75–78
alternative hedonism 26–27, 31
armchair travel 29, 31
ASMR (Autonomous Sensory Meridian Response) videos 75–78, 80
aspirational labour 43, 46–47, 51–55
audience labour 43, 55–58
audio triggers 68, 75, 76

baking, cultural connotations of 68, 77
Beer, Maggie 25
Best Leftovers Ever! (Netflix) 42, 51, 55, 59
Beyer, Nicole 56
Blumenthal, Heston 42
brand machines 68, 78, 79, 80
Bryant, Simon 25

cable television 1, 4, 18, 20, 21, 43, 47, 87
Cake Wars 42
Cake Wars (Food Network) 42

catch-up television 19, 22–23, 28–29
celebrity: for reality TV contestants 46–47, 50; self-branding and 51; YouTube-specific celebrity 70
celebrity chefs: influence of COVID-19 pandemic on TV programs 87–88; relationship with audience 90; role 70
Channel 4, UK 27, 28, 42, 88
climate crisis, meat consumption and 32–34
Clooney, George 35
content aggregators 65
content creation, success in 51–52, 56, 70, 71–72
The Cook and the Chef (ABC TV) 24, 25
Cooked with Cannabis (Netflix) 42, 51, 55, 59
cookery-educative programs 4
Cooking Tree (YouTube channel) 76–77, 80, 81
co-presence 88, 96, 97
COVID-19 pandemic: impact on broadcast food television 87–89; impact on broadcast television 87; opportunities offered by 104–105; role of television during 98–99
Crazy Delicious (Netflix): diversity of participants 49; format 42, 47; framing of contestants 51–52, 54; as loving reality 47–51; passionate work 52–53
Cupcake Wars (Food Network, US) 42

114 Index

digital flow 34–36
digital food cultures 4–6
digital food media, vital capacities 74
digital food porn 3
digital food studies, approach to digital food media 2–3
digital food TV: political potentialities of 105; politics of 3–4, 10, 12, 108–110; potential to generate affective engagements 89
digital television, distinguished from 'legacy' television 87

Easy Meals for Every Day (Channel 4, UK) 89, 101–113, 104, 105
eating: and affect 71–75; nascent and contingent forms of 73
eco-reality television 11, 26, 31
Ekstedt, Niklas 42
environmental concerns 26, 27, 28, 31
Epic Meal Time (YouTube) 7
escape, politics of 28–32
Escape to River Cottage see River Cottage series (Channel 4, UK)
Evans, Matthew 19, 26, 27, 28, 29–30, 32–33, 35

Facebook 2, 12, 65–66, 71, 79, 81, 87
farmers' markets 24
Fearnely-Whittingstall, Hugh 18, 26, 27, 28, 29–30, 32–33, 35
Feimster, Fortune 49
flow 19, 20–23, 31, 34–36
food media studies 2, 5, 67
Food Network 42, 43
food television: armchair travel 29; capacity to connect to larger-scale concerns 23–24, 26; historical specificity of 23, 34; history 1–2, 4–6; 'softly, softly' politics 30, 31; tensions between ordinary and aspirational 91; *see also* post-network food television
food television studies: challenges of post-network food television 6–10; interest in digital food 5
food tourism 29
food travelogues 29, 30, 31
For the Love of Meat (documentary) 32

Gok Cooks Chinese 31
the 'good life,' reimagining 23–28
Goodwin, Julie 45
Gourmet Farmer (SBS TV): alternative hedonism 26–27, 31–32; broadcast on catch-up TV 19; as food travelogue 29, 30, 31, 34; livestock rearing 32–33; ratings success 19; reading the politics of 18, 25–28, 30–32, 36; valorising of traditional food practices 29–30
The Great British Bake Off 42, 49, 50, 54
green lifestyle television 26, 31, 33, 34, 35

The Hairy Bikers Food Tour of Britain 24
Hairy Bikers' Mississippi Adventure 31
Hall, Carla 42
Hugh's Chicken Run (culinary documentary) 27, 32
Hugh's Fat Fight (culinary documentary) 35
Hugh's War on Waste (culinary documentary) 35
Hussain, Nadiya 49, 50

industrial food systems, concerns about 24–26, 32–34
Instagram 2, 51–52, 56, 87
instructional television 4, 69–71
intimacy, television as medium of 89–91

Jamie's Food Revolution 94
Jamie's Great Italian Escape 29

Keep Cooking and Carry On (Channel 4, UK): broadcasting of 88, 91; contrasted with *Easy Meals* 101–103, 104; digital production techniques 88, 89; drawing viewers close 94–101; at-home filming 88, 94–95; messaging during the COVID-19 pandemic 92–94; production 88; social media comments on 96, 100–101; studio episodes 92–94
Kitchen Nightmares 29

Index   115

Lawson, Nigella 4, 35, 70, 90
Liaw, Adam 45
lifestyle cookery programs 4, 5, 23–28, 30–32, 86
lifestyle television 4, 5, 21, 23, 26, 91, 102–103
Local Heroes 29
loving reality 43, 47–51, 59

March, Holden 42
marketing, YouTube channels 70, 81
MasterChef 45, 47, 48, 49, 51, 54, 59
MasterChef Australia 7
MCNs (multichannel networks) 65
meat consumption, and the climate crisis 32–34
MetDaan Cakes 65, 71, 75, 81
My Kitchen Rules 47–48, 54

Nailed It! (Netflix) 42, 51, 55, 56, 59
The Naked Chef 91
The Naked Chef (BBC Two) 4, 29
NBC 20
Nelson, Candace 42, 43
neoliberal pedagogy, reality television and 43–47, 54
Nerdy Nummies (YouTube channel) 69–70
Netflix: largest markets 42, 60n1; recommendation system 59; scholarship on impact of 5–6
Netflix food programming: as ambient TV 41; comforting, uplifting quality of 41–42; compared to broadcast and cable TV 47; competition reality programs 42; exploitation of contestants and audience labour 55–56; originally produced content 1, 41, 42; politics of streaming reality 58–59

Oliver, Jamie: critiques of cookery programs 94; *Easy Meals for Every Day* 89, 101–103, 104, 105; as family man 90, 95–97; first cookery program 4; *Jamie's Food Revolution* 94; *Jamie's Great Italian Escape* 29; lifestylisation of cookery programs 4, 70, 91, 101; *The Naked Chef* 4, 29, 91; relationship with audience 90–91; *see also Keep Cooking and Carry On* (Channel 4, UK)
Oliver, Jools 95, 98
Oliver, River 95, 96, 98, 102; lifestylisation of cookery programs 102–103
on-demand viewing 23
online food videos: advertising 80; affect switches 79–81; AMR-inspired videos 76–78; continuities with earlier media forms 69–71; eating affect 71–75; marketing opportunities 80; nascent and contingent forms of cooking 73–74; political analysis of 82–83; proliferation 65; significance and brand value 80–82; textual analysis 67–68, 71; users' engagement with 66–67, 72–73; vitalities and visceralities 82–83

Pansino, Rosanna 69–70, 75
passionate work 52–53
politics-as-pleasure 27, 35
Pollan, Michael 24, 32
post-network food television, challenges for food TV scholarship 6–10
produce, sourcing of 24–25
product placement 80

Ramsay, Gordon 29
reality television 9, 20; advertising tropes 48; context of emergence 44; cooking competition formats 45–46; eco-reality television 11, 26, 31; excess of affect 48; loving reality 43, 47–51, 59; makeover genre 44, 45, 46, 48; and neoliberal pedagogy 43–47, 54; payoffs for participants/contestants 50; politics of streaming reality 58–60; scholarly understandings of 44; work of 46–47
reruns of older programs, temporality and 20–23
River Cottage series (Channel 4, UK): alternative hedonism 26–27, 31–32; broadcast on catch-up TV 19; *Escape to River Cottage* 25, 26; first airing of 18, 25; as food

travelogue 29, 30, 31, 34; livestock rearing 32–33; as ratings hit 18–19; reading the politics of 25–28, 30–32, 36; *Tales from River Cottage* 31; valorising of traditional food practices 29–30
Rosie's Dessert Spot (YouTube channel) 71–72, 75, 80, 81

SBS: Charter 22; ratings successes 19
SBS On Demand: advertising 34–35; food programming 19, 22, 29, 31, 35–36; production dates of programs 23, 28
Schwarzenegger, Arnold 97
Seinfeld (sit-com) 20
self-branding 45–47, 50, 51, 52, 57
self-sufficiency 26, 28, 30
smart bottles 78–79
Sourced 31
stand-and-stir formats 1, 4, 69
Stein, Rick 29
streaming television: algorithmic logics 59; politics of streaming reality 58–60; temporality 22–23, 28; unpaid and underpaid labour 57–58
Sugar Rush (Netflix): diversity of participants 49; format 42–43, 47; framing of contestants 52–53, 54; as loving reality 47–51
sustainability 26, 27, 30, 31, 32

Taste the Nation with Padma Lakshmi 31
Tastemade 65
Tasty 65, 72, 73–74, 80, 81
television: cable television 1, 4, 18, 20, 21, 43, 47, 87; catch-up television 19, 22–23, 28–29; digital TV distinguished from 'legacy' TV 87; eco-reality television 11, 26, 31; foodie boom 23; lifestyle television 4, 5, 20, 23; as mass medium 7; as medium of intimacy 89–91, 97; operation as a cusp formation 88–89, 94, 97, 99, 103, 109; *see also* reality television; traditional broadcast television
television industry, and YouTube 3
television studies 5–6, 8, 9–10
televisual flow 19, 20–23, 31, 34–36
textual analysis 7–8, 10–11, 57, 67–68, 71
TikTok 1, 87
Torres, Jacques 56
traditional broadcast television: advertising 8, 20, 34; food programming compared to Netflix 47; food programming compared to YouTube channels 69–79; impact of COVID-19 pandemic 87–88
Turland, Guy 31
Twitter 2, 100

visual triggers 68, 75, 76

What's the Catch? (culinary documentary) 35
whiteness, market value of 56
Williams, Raymond 19, 20, 34
work: aspirational labour 43, 46–47, 51–55; audience labour 43, 55–58; invisiblisation of 43; passionate work 52–53; reframing of 51–55; work-as-leisure 43, 51–55

YouTube: carnivalesque food videos 3; commercial, algorithmic logics 79; marketing 70, 81; parallels between food channels and traditional food TV 69–70; and television industry 3

Zumbo, Adriano 42